The Job-Seekers' Bible

by

Lawrence E. Barlow, M.A.

A
VCA
Publication

Post Office Box 1566
Lakeside, California 92040-0950

ISBN 0-940150-00-X

Copyright© 1981, 1986 by Lawrence E. Barlow

Printed in the United States of America

Seventh Printing 1988

Library of Congress Cataloging in Publication Data

Barlow, Lawrence E. (Lawrence Edward), 1941-
  The job-seekers' bible.

  Summary: A guide to finding and keeping a job, with discussions of employment qualifications, applications, openings, interviews, resumes, and recommendations.
  2. Job hunting. (1. Job hunting. 2. Vocational guidance)
I. Title.
HF5382.7.B37   650.1'4   81-11494
ISBN 0-940150-00-X   AACR2

Dedication

This book is dedicated to ordinary people . . .
people who work or *want to work* for a living.

Acknowledgments

THANKS to all those ordinary people who participated and gained
employment as a result of the many Job Search Training
Seminars.

THANKS to all those employers who afforded time and effort in
verifying practical job-seeking strategies.

THANKS to those laymen and laywomen, business persons, and
professionals who critiqued the original manuscript.

THANKS to Barbara A. Morrison for the professional application
of her typographical talents.

THANKS to Cheryl Gilman for the artistic conceptualization and
creation of the book design.

THANKS to Alex Brown for the stimulating bookcover illustration.

THANKS to Joyce Ercoli–Barlow, who for four years encouraged
the idea and edited to realization...
THE JOB-SEEKERS' BIBLE.

Preface

CONGRATULATIONS! Beginning to read this book indicates that you are motivated and interested in improving your job and/or career status. This is the first step to:

(1) Greater earning power;
(2) More enjoyable working conditions; and
(3) Job security.

If you are like most people, you probably do not know exactly HOW to begin this improvement. Schools have attempted to train you in the academics . . . but when did anyone ever give you information regarding TECHNIQUES for job hunting and job retention? Perhaps never!

A good job is the key to making good money. The key TECHNIQUE to getting that good job is successful job interviewing. This book will teach you TECHNIQUES and give you TOOLS necessary for "landing" that good job. Your CONFIDENCE will be developed as you learn how to "play the game" by being prepared and having answers to those questions asked during an interview.

This easy-to-read book is the key that will unlock the door to thousands of dollars for YOU!

Table of Contents

How To Use This Book

It seems strange that a person will expend in excess of 200 hours on a one-semester literature course but will give virtually no time to career selection. This "bible" is designed to be read in two to three hours and will be worth thousands of dollars to you.

Read the book from cover to cover . . . then go back and select those TECHNIQUES and TOOLS personally needed BEFORE you go for the job you want. The TECHNIQUES and TOOLS are variable and should be based on your own personality and desires. One of the TECHNIQUES and/or TOOLS may be all you need for that good job or you may need to implement all of them.

This book is written in a style you can easily read and understand. Humor is injected throughout to make your reading not only financially beneficial but personally enjoyable. This book is written in context with reality . . . that is, the TECHNIQUES and TOOLS have been field-proven by thousands of people (just like yourself) who have attained employment using them.

Some people have difficulty with theory and abstract logic but everyone can learn to use TECHNIQUES and TOOLS. SO CAN YOU! In fact, it is so simple to learn that many people feel foolish for having struggled with job-seeking so long without realizing there is an easy way.

Use this book . . . write in it . . . wear it out . . . for, like an old pair of shoes, it will make you comfortable only after you have used it. Take it with you when you go for your job interview so you can have a reminder of the CONFIDENCE you had when you read it.

And now . . . BEGIN . . . and . . . ENJOY!

CHAPTER 1

Misconceptions

EDUCATIONAL REQUIREMENTS

College Graduates
Non-Skilled Workers
Skilled Workers

TYPES OF JOBS AVAILABLE

WORTH

CAREER/JOB-CHANGING

CAREER/JOB CONTENTMENT

JOB SECURITY

Misconceptions

MISCONCEPTION #1
Educational Requirements

JOBS FOR COLLEGE GRADUATES
(Four years or more)

Approximately 15% of all jobs in the United States require a college degree. That is to say, only 15 out of each 100 jobs require at least graduation from a four-year college.

If you do not have a four-year college degree you still have the option of selecting a job from the 85% that is available to you . . . now, isn't that nice to know!

Although individuals with a degree tend to make more money in a lifetime, *all* college graduates do not make a lot of money. Doctors, lawyers, engineers, etc. tend to do well financially while teachers, social workers and musicians tend to fall lower on the salary scale. Since you will be selecting a job on the basis of your likes and dislikes AS WELL AS financial rewards, these concepts will be considered later in this book.

THE NON-SKILLED WORKER

Approximately 5% of all jobs require no skill and/or no schooling. You can learn to do this kind of work in about two minutes. The pay in some of these jobs is good (trash collectors in a large city can earn $25,000 a year), but most of these non-skilled jobs only pay minimum wage.

Of all the different classes or types of jobs that exist, the non-skilled has the highest occurrence of nervous disorders related to the job (ulcers, heartburn, insomnia, nervousness, etc.). The frustration lies in the fact that the worker can be replaced immediately . . . thus the worker has no job security . . . anybody can perform the non-skilled job.

THE SKILLED WORKER (Technical)

Approximately 80% of all jobs in the United States require some learned skill or technical training. Technical jobs require from two weeks to three years of training to gain "entry level skills." (Entry level skills are those learned skills necessary to get a job in a particular technical area.)

Some examples of jobs that fall into this category are as follows (approximate training time and entry level wage estimate):

Job Title	Training Time	Wage Range (hourly)		
Vocational Nurse	one year	$5.00	to	$ 7.50
Welder	six months	$4.50	to	$ 8.00
Secretary	six months	$4.00	to	$ 6.00
Electronic Assembler	two months	$4.00	to	$ 6.00
Auto Tune Up	nine months	$4.00	to	$ 8.00
Salesperson	one week to one year	$3.50	to	$50.00
Mechanical Engineer	four years	$8.00	to	$13.00
Bookkeeper	one year	$4.50	to	$ 7.00
Police Officer	four months	$5.75	to	$ 8.00
Teacher	four years	$6.50	to	$ 9.00

In the past, companies would train individuals for entry level jobs. In today's economically competitive society, employers expect potential employees to have entry level skills. Once a company has you as an employee, they will upgrade your skills as they advance you.

Since 80 out of every 100 available jobs are in the technically skilled area, your chances of employment in this area are the highest.

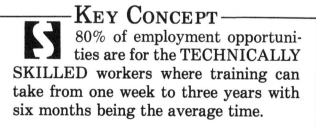

KEY CONCEPT

80% of employment opportunities are for the TECHNICALLY SKILLED workers where training can take from one week to three years with six months being the average time.

MISCONCEPTION #2
Types of Jobs Available

Did you know there are over 20,000 different types of jobs available to you?

Most people limit their job choice to chance. They choose a job because "that is what everyone else does," or "it was the first thing that came along." The D.O.T. (Dictionary of Occupational Titles, United States Department of Labor, Employment and Training Administration, Fourth Edition, 1977) lists and describes over *20,000* types of jobs to choose from. You may want to look over this dictionary that can be found in most public libraries.

KEY CONCEPT

You have a choice of over 20,000 types of jobs. Research, investigate and/or get vocational counseling if need be. KNOW THE JOB YOU WANT AND GO FOR IT!

MISCONCEPTION #3
Worth

The 1985 average yearly salary for a worker in the United States was approximately $16,640. Now there are some workers who earn more . . . and some less.

Take a look at the amount of money over a lifetime (10,000 working days) that just 50¢ more an hour can make:

Current Earnings	Per	Earnings After 50¢ Increase
$ 8.00	hour	$ 8.50
320.00	week	340.00
1,386.67	month	1,473.33
16,640.00	year	17,680.00

If you subtract $16,640.00 (current earnings per year) from $17,680.00 (earnings after 50¢ per hour increase per year), a net gain of $1,040.00 exists.

Let's go one step further. If you multiply $1,040.00 (increased earnings over a year at 50¢ more per hour) by 40 (average number of working years in a person's life), you experience a net gain of $41,600.00. Can you think of any ways to spend $41,600.00?

KEY CONCEPT

Select the job at the wage you want because your worth adds up substantially over your lifetime!

MISCONCEPTION #4
Career/Job-Changing

Statistics indicate that you will change jobs at least ten times in your life . . . included in this are career changes.

Job attainment skills (where and how to look for work, how to interview and follow-up, etc.) are important assets to those who will switch jobs. Often a job switch will be an advancement in both pay and status.

Avoid being trapped by the old mentality that implies you should have the same job for the rest of your life. In the 1950's this was true, but today's modern technological society often forces job changes on an individual. After you have finished this book, you will have developed the CONFIDENCE and TECHNIQUES needed to change jobs as often as need be.

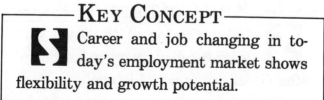

KEY CONCEPT

Career and job changing in today's employment market shows flexibility and growth potential.

MISCONCEPTION #5
Career / Job Contentment

Are all people happy in their jobs? NO! Surveys indicate that 80% of the working public are not happy with their jobs.

Most people don't realize that they give about ten hours per day to their job (not including overtime). Take a look at an example day:

Time	Activity	Allotted Hours		
		Work	Personal	Sleep
7:00 a.m. - 7:30 a.m.	Rise and eat breakfast		0.5	
7:30 a.m. - 8:00 a.m.	Drive to work	0.5		
8:00 a.m. - 12:00 noon	Work	4.0		
12:00 noon - 12:30 p.m.	Lunch (at work)	0.5		
12:30 p.m. - 4:30 p.m.	Work	4.0		
4:30 p.m. - 5:00 p.m.	Drive home	0.5		
5:00 p.m. - 5:30 p.m.	Next work day preparation (Work clothes, personal needs, etc.)	0.5		
5:30 p.m. - 11:00 p.m.	Personal time		5.5	
11:00 p.m. - 7:00 a.m.	Sleep			8.0
		10.0	6.0	8.0

Your day may vary from the example given, but probably not much. If you dislike your job, you have about ten hours of dissatisfaction to live with and only six hours to recover. Since most of our waking hours involve working for an employer, the importance of wise job selection becomes obvious.

Whatever job you perform must be appropriate to your interests, aptitudes (learning abilities), and temperament. The company must have your respect, trust and confidence in order for you to be happy during the entire work day.

By gaining job-changing CONFIDENCE and TECHNIQUES, leaving an undesirable job situation will not be a fearsome experience.

A successful, middle-aged, employed male dreads his job. He earns about $30,000 a year and cannot wait to retire . . . if he lives that long.

A 30-year-old female machine operator (lathe, drill press, mill, etc.) is so excited about her job that she cannot wait to get there. She makes about $15,000 a year.

Which would you rather be?

KEY CONCEPT

62% of your waking hours is devoted to your employment. Get the job that not only pays well, but gives personal satisfaction . . . for your own sake and for the sake of those around you.

MISCONCEPTION #6
Job Security

Job security lies in the person . . . not the company.

Job security lies in your skills, and your ability to exchange those skills for dollars. CONFIDENCE in yourself affords more job security than confidence in a company that will "be around forever."

Several nationally known corporations have come close to shutting down. It is good to be an employee for a company, develop friends, advance, etc. . . . but do not be lulled to sleep. No job is absolutely secure . . . just more secure than a risky one.

Your ability to sell yourself and your skills will give you the CONFIDENCE necessary to make good money, enjoy your work, and not worry about job security.

KEY CONCEPT

Job security lies in you, your skills, ability and confidence . . . not in a company.

SUMMARY

You now have a true concept of the way it is in the job market. This brief and specific approach to clarify misconceptions will assist you in developing the TECHNIQUES and TOOLS to get the job you want.

CHAPTER 2

Know Thyself

AWARENESS TECHNIQUES

Strengths
Weaknesses
Likes
Dislikes
Personal Needs

Know Thyself

We all have desirable qualities and undesirable qualities. We all have strengths that can contribute to a job or weaknesses that can detract from it. The important factor is that you recognize yours . . . before a prospective employer does.

If you will learn about yourself . . . that is, "know thyself," you will be able to convey just enough about yourself to others without giving away all of your weak points. Knowing personal weak points and strong points will enable you to do better in the job market.

The AWARENESS TECHNIQUES in this chapter will help you learn about yourself in relation to the job market.

AWARENESS TECHNIQUE A:
Are You . . .

DIRECTIONS:

Check (✓) the appropriate box for the following.
Use the dictionary to look up the meaning of any word you are unsure of.

ARE YOU . . .	YES	NO	UNSURE
Accountable?	☐	☐	☐
Able to adapt to most situations?	☐	☐	☐
Aggressive?	☐	☐	☐
Alert to problems?	☐	☐	☐
Assertive?	☐	☐	☐
Competitive?	☐	☐	☐
Confident of yourself?	☐	☐	☐
Considerate of other people?	☐	☐	☐
Creative?	☐	☐	☐
A decision maker?	☐	☐	☐
A dependable person?	☐	☐	☐
Energetic?	☐	☐	☐
Enthusiastic?	☐	☐	☐
Friendly?	☐	☐	☐
A follower?	☐	☐	☐
Hard working?	☐	☐	☐
Honest?	☐	☐	☐
Innovative?	☐	☐	☐
A leader?	☐	☐	☐
A listener?	☐	☐	☐
Loyal to a cause?	☐	☐	☐
Mature?	☐	☐	☐
Organized?	☐	☐	☐
People-oriented?	☐	☐	☐
A polite person?	☐	☐	☐
Practical?	☐	☐	☐
Punctual (on time)?	☐	☐	☐
Trustworthy?	☐	☐	☐
Well-groomed?	☐	☐	☐

AWARENESS TECHNIQUE B:
Do You . . .

DIRECTIONS:

Check (✔) the appropriate box for the following.

Use the dictionary to look up the meaning of any word you are unsure of.

DO YOU . . .	YES	NO	UNSURE
Communicate well?	☐	☐	☐
Concentrate well?	☐	☐	☐
Cooperate with people?	☐	☐	☐
Delegate authority?	☐	☐	☐
Follow directions?	☐	☐	☐
Have high standards?	☐	☐	☐
Identify problems?	☐	☐	☐
Have a good imagination?	☐	☐	☐
Have integrity?	☐	☐	☐
Complete tasks?	☐	☐	☐
Plan ahead?	☐	☐	☐
Like to solve problems?	☐	☐	☐

AWARENESS TECHNIQUE C:
Can You . . .

DIRECTIONS:

Check (✓) the appropriate box for the following.

Use the dictionary to look up the meaning of any word you are unsure of.

CAN YOU . . .	YES	NO	UNSURE
Manage other people?	☐	☐	☐
Meet given deadlines?	☐	☐	☐
Motivate other people?	☐	☐	☐
Get motivated by other people?	☐	☐	☐
Discuss situations (negotiate)?	☐	☐	☐
Persuade people?	☐	☐	☐
Be resourceful?	☐	☐	☐
Be responsible?	☐	☐	☐
Be a self-starter?	☐	☐	☐
Be understanding?	☐	☐	☐
Work under pressure?	☐	☐	☐

Now review AWARENESS TECHNIQUES A, B, and C. Are you beginning to know yourself better?

PERSONAL NEEDS

Personal needs are demands each individual has and vary greatly from person to person.

Some people need to have prestige and fame while others need to be alone and private. Some people must have a white collar job while others enjoy working with their hands.

Many of us never have stopped long enough to determine our needs as they exist relative to a job. Since a job takes up about 62% of our "awake" hours*, securing a job that meets our needs is most important.

The following AWARENESS TECHNIQUES will help you determine your personal needs regarding employment.

---

*See Chapter 1 — MISCONCEPTION #5 — KEY CONCEPT

AWARENESS TECHNIQUE D:
Priorities

DIRECTIONS:

Mark the five most important items to you when selecting a job. Rank them 1 - 2 - 3 - 4 - 5 with choice #1 being the most important and choice #5 being the least important to you:

____ enjoyment	____ emotional satisfaction
____ job security	____ glamour
____ safe working conditions	____ importance of job
____ retirement plans	____ spousal or family approval
____ insurance programs	____ use of natural ability
____ time off - vacations - holidays	____ fulfillment of what is expected
____ rate of pay	____ convenience (near home)
____ ability to use training	____ advancement opportunities
____ likeable fellow-workers	____ friendly boss

AWARENESS TECHNIQUE E:
Preferred Work Situations

DIRECTIONS:

Check (✔) the ONE type of work situation which you would prefer in each given choice:

☐ repetitive tasks	or	☐	varied tasks
☐ work in a group	or	☐	work alone
☐ outdoor work	or	☐	indoor work
☐ public contact (sales/service)	or	☐	no direct public contact
☐ have close supervision	or	☐	work independently
☐ physically active work	or	☐	mostly sitting
☐ day shift	or	☐	night shift
☐ math/reading skills required	or	☐	mechanical skills required
☐ be your own boss	or	☐	supervised by someone else
☐ have set schedules to meet	or	☐	no specific time deadlines
☐ routine/detailed work	or	☐	creative work

AWARENESS TECHNIQUE F:
Favorite School Subjects

DIRECTIONS:

Mark five of your favorite school subjects ranking them 1 - 2 - 3 - 4 - 5 with #1 being the most favorite and #5 being the least favorite. Write examples when necessary.

____ English: _____

____ Math: _____

____ Drafting: _____

____ Music: _____

____ Art: _____

____ Home Economics: _____

____ Physical Education: _____

____ Agriculture: _____

____ Science: _____

____ Shop: _____

____ Business: _____

____ Others: _____

AWARENESS TECHNIQUE G:
Hobbies

DIRECTIONS:

List your favorite hobbies and/or leisure time activities in order of importance:

1. _____

2. _____

3. _____

4. _____

5. _____

6. _____

7. _____

8. _____

AWARENESS TECHNIQUE H:
Dream Sheet

DIRECTIONS:

If you could apply for various jobs listed in the newspaper (even if you are not qualified), which would you choose? Why?

1. _____

   Why? _____

2. _____

   Why? _____

3. _____

   Why? _____

4. _____

   Why? _____

5. _____

   Why? _____

6. _____

   Why? _____

7. _____

   Why _____

8. _____

   Why? _____

AWARENESS TECHNIQUE I:
Jobs

DIRECTIONS:

List the jobs you are thinking about applying for right now.

1. _____
2. _____
3. _____
4. _____
5. _____
6. _____
7. _____
8. _____

AWARENESS TECHNIQUE J:
Training

DIRECTIONS:

If you could go to school for extra training, what area(s) or class(es) would you take?

1. _____
2. _____
3. _____
4. _____
5. _____
6. _____
7. _____
8. _____

AWARENESS TECHNIQUE K:
Pay

DIRECTIONS:
List how much pay (per hour or per month) you would need from a job.

1. $ _____ per hour

2. $ _____ per month

3. $ _____ I don't know

AWARENESS TECHNIQUE L:
Personal Traits

DIRECTIONS:
Mark an X in the box nearest the characteristic that best describes you as a person.

good health	☐	☐	☐	☐	☐	poor health
outgoing	☐	☐	☐	☐	☐	reserved
makes own decisions	☐	☐	☐	☐	☐	decisions made for you
organized	☐	☐	☐	☐	☐	disorganized
experienced work record	☐	☐	☐	☐	☐	little work experience
assertive	☐	☐	☐	☐	☐	submissive
persistent	☐	☐	☐	☐	☐	impatient

AWARENESS TECHNIQUE M:
Difficulties

DIRECTIONS:

List any problems or situations that you could foresee as difficult to put up with or handle on a job.

1. _____

2. _____

3. _____

4. _____

5. _____

6. _____

7. _____

8. _____

AWARENESS TECHNIQUE N:
Ideal Job

DIRECTIONS:

List your personal preference for the ideal job.

Ideal type of work: _____

Ideal location: _____

Ideal type boss: _____

Ideal hours: _____

Others: _____

SUMMARY

Many of you know who you are and what you want. Setting goals (deciding what you want) and considering your likes and dislikes (knowing who you are) will allow you to choose a job, not just accept any kind of work.

During a job interview you must know yourself well enough so you can respond to questions in a manner that makes you look good. During the entire interview you must impress the employer positively by emphasizing your strong points.

The AWARENESS TECHNIQUES in this chapter have helped you to know yourself better so that you can make better impressions and decisions.

Knowing what you want is the key to getting what you want.

CHAPTER 3

Trick Questions

RESPONSE TECHNIQUES

General
Technical
Past Employment

Trick Questions

During an employment interview an applicant was asked, "Tell me about yourself." The applicant proceeded to do just that. It was like a true confession . . . telling about intimate parts of his personal life that had nothing to do with the job.

Prospective employers will often ask a variety of questions. They often use "trick" questions to see how you react — thereby getting insight into your personality and ability to deal with difficult situations. These questions usually force the applicant to answer quickly and with little thought. If you know your weak and strong points you will be better able to answer those questions in a manner that is appropriate to your personality. A natural response is your aim. YOU WILL BE HIRED PRIMARILY BECAUSE THE COMPANY LIKES YOU . . . your skills are secondary. Your personality traits and attitudes are measured during trick questions to determine if you will "fit in well" with the rest of the company employees.

A series of TRICK QUESTION RESPONSE TECHNIQUES follow for your practice.

RESPONSE TECHNIQUE A:
Trick Questions — General

DIRECTIONS:

The following statements are trick questions most asked by prospective employers. Good and Poor responses are listed. You should write a response that fits your personality . . . a response that will persuade them to LIKE you . . . and HIRE you.

QUESTION #1:   *"What can I do for you?"*

Poor Response: "Ahh . . . I guess I want a job."

GOOD Response: "I would like to interview for a ma-chinist position in your company."

KEY CONCEPT

Name a specific job or jobs. State the specific job you desire to have with the company.

Your Response:_____

_____

_____

_____

_____

_____

_____

QUESTION #2: *"Why do you want this job?"*

Poor Response: "It is the only one open."

GOOD Response: "I am interested in this type of work and have had experience in this area."

KEY CONCEPT

The good response shows that you are an intelligent person who can make decisions.

Your Response:_____

_____

_____

_____

_____

_____

_____

_____

QUESTION #3:   *"Tell me about yourself..."*

Poor Response: "I have four children. I am in the
                   process of getting a divorce and
                   need to go to work. My husband is a
                   real problem ... he hasn't ..." etc.,
                   etc.

GOOD Response: "I am an even-tempered person
                   who doesn't get upset easily. I have
                   always made friends readily ..."
                   etc.

KEY CONCEPT

S Always refer to yourself in a positive fashion. Never refer to a
weak point. NEVER TALK MORE
THAN ONE MINUTE. (Turn your watch
on your wrist so you can see it without being too conspicuous and time yourself with
the second hand. No family skeletons, deodorant failures, or sex life details, please!)

Your Response:_____

_____

_____

_____

_____

_____

QUESTION #4:   *"What would your last supervisor say about you?"*

Poor Response: "He ... ah ... he would say that he fired me because I was always late ... but he was all wrong 'cause I was only late four times."

GOOD Response: "He would say that I was a good worker, well-organized, loyal, but late to work on occasion. I have a more reliable car now and have resolved the late problem."

KEY CONCEPT
Tell the truth in all cases BUT emphasize your good points FIRST, then (if you must) touch on a weak point and illustrate how you are improving. You need not tell everything about a weak point. Say just enough to show you are human and can make mistakes, but intelligent enough to correct them.

Your Response:_____ _____

_____

_____

_____

_____

QUESTION #5:   *"What kind of people irritate you?"*

Poor Response: "People who disrupt my schedule or
                   think they know it all really get me
                   mad."

GOOD Response: "Generally people do not irritate me
                   to the point where I become nonpro-
                   ductive, but continued interrup-
                   tions in my productivity tend to
                   annoy me."

KEY CONCEPT

Being blunt in the interview implies a quick temper. Being diplo-
matic but truthful implies controlled
behavior patterns under stress. This is a
desirable quality.

Your Response:_____

_____

_____

_____

_____

_____

_____

_____

QUESTION #6:   *"Why should I hire you?"*

Poor Response: "Because I am perfect for the job."

GOOD Response: "Because I want the job and have the skills necessary to perform it well. I will work hard and put out my best effort to learn new concepts. "

KEY CONCEPT

During the interview you are a salesperson . . . you are selling YOURSELF. If you imply perfection, it sounds foolish . . . if you indicate effort and performance, you sound promising.

Your Response:_____

_____

_____

_____

_____

_____

_____

_____

_____

QUESTION #7:   *"What would you do if... a custom-
                  er told you to go to hell?"* (or any
                  other given stress situation related
                  to the particular job you are apply-
                  ing for)

Poor Response: "I would tell them to leave the
                  store."

GOOD Response: "I would imagine that your com-
                  pany has a policy for dealing with
                  angry customers. I would probably
                  follow the policy or suggest that the
                  person see the manager."

KEY CONCEPT

Show your flexibility in your answer if possible. If a "firm" answer is required because of a law or stat-ute, you should still respond in a flexible manner and cite the given law.

Your Response:_____

_____

_____

_____

_____

_____

QUESTION #8:   *"Don't you think you are over-qualified for this job?*

Poor Response: "No, I am not that overqualified."

                              or

"So what?"

GOOD Response: "It is true that I am highly qualified. However, I adapt well, work hard, and am eager to use my qualifications to your best advantage."

KEY CONCEPT

Give the employer the impression that you are aware of the problems that could result from hiring an overqualified person, but that you are adaptable enough to avoid problems. Impress the employer with your adaptablity and ability to work hard.

Your Response:_____

_____

_____

_____

_____

QUESTION #9:   *"Don't you think you are under-qualified for this job?"*

Poor Response: "Everybody has to start some-place."

                                    or

                   "Ahh . . . uh . . . I guess you're right."

GOOD Response: "I may not have all of the qualifica-tions that you desire, but I am a quick learner and a hard worker. Because I am motivated I would be an asset to your company."

KEY CONCEPT

Always impress the interviewer with your ability to learn and work hard. Often good workers are hired regardless of limited qualifications.

Your Response:_____

_____

_____

_____

_____

_____

QUESTION #10:   *"Do you have any questions?"*

Poor Response: "No, I know everything there is to know."

GOOD Response: "Right now I cannot think of any questions, but may I call you back if any arise?"

KEY CONCEPT

Again, never imply that you know everything, but imply that you are interested enough to think about the job and interview after you leave. The good response also provides the option to call the interviewer again.

Your Response:_____

_____

_____

_____

_____

_____

_____

_____

_____

_____

RESPONSE TECHNIQUE B:
Trick Questions — Technical

Questions regarding technical aspects of a job may be asked during the interview. A specific answer may be given if you are sure you know the correct answer. If you are not absolutely positive, it is better to respond in a manner that illustrates your ability to find out where the answer is located.

QUESTION #11:   (to a potential secretary) *"How many typing elements are there for the IBM Electronic Typewriter?"*

Poor Response: "Ahh . . . eee . . . three?"

or

"How am I supposed to know that?"

GOOD Response: "I am sure it is in the neighborhood of twenty . . . but I could call the IBM Company and easily find out the exact number."

── KEY CONCEPT ──
If you are not sure of the answer, indicate you know where to find the answer.

Your Response:_____

_____

_____

_____

RESPONSE TECHNIQUE C:
Trick Questions — Past Employment

Questions regarding past employment and past employers often come up during the interview. Always respond positively to your past employment experiences even if they were not very positive. The interviewer may ultimately be one of your past employers and your responses may someday include him. Your response here is important.

QUESTION #12:   *"Tell me about your last employer."*

Poor Response: "He was really a turkey. He was always late for work and really came down hard on his workers when they were late. He had other problems, too . . ." etc., etc.

GOOD Response: "The company was demanding but I conformed and met the requirements. Currently I am interested in change and advancement."

KEY CONCEPT

Be positive about past employment but indicate the desire for change and advancement.

Your Response:_____

_____

_____

_____

SUMMARY

Trick questions during the interview are intended to catch you off guard . . . to force you to uncover your real personality. The answers are not what the interviewer desires . . . your reaction is what he or she is after.

The following is a list of possible trick questions. By now you should be able to respond with relative ease.

1. *Why did you apply at this company?*
2. *Where do you anticipate to be in three years?*
3. *Why did you select this kind of work?*
4. *Have you ever been fired?*
5. *Why have you been unemployed all this time?*
6. *What did you like best about your last job?*
7. *What did you like least about your last job?*
8. *Why did you change career fields?*

To make your answers less blunt, you can add a "probably," "sometimes," or "maybe." Feel free to ask for clarification if the question is too misleading or vague.

Knowing yourself is half the battle . . . anticipating and reacting positively to trick questions will enable a victory!

CHAPTER 4

Questionable Questions

RESPONSE TECHNIQUES

Illegal Questions
Special Techniques for the Ex-Offender

Questionable Questions

You may find business people who do not know how to interview an applicant and/or do not care about the laws regarding an applicant's privacy during an employment interview.

Laws exist that are supposed to protect your privacy as a job applicant. Prospective employers are often unaware of these laws or just do not obey them.

Questions regarding race, marital status, national origin, religion, age and handicaps are considered illegal and should not be asked. If a potential employer asks you questionable questions, be sure to have a good response ready. Determine your response in relation to what you perceive the interviewer's intentions to be. He or she may be a benevolent, hard-working, business person who is interested in you and ignorant of the law (a good person to work for) or he or she may be a hard-driving executive who does not care about the law or about you.

If an interviewer asks you a question that is inappropriate or illegal, your response should reflect your skills, qualifications, experience, flexibility, and potential, and not just your knowledge of the law. You may even answer an illegal question but know ahead of time just how you will handle the situation.

The following RESPONSE TECHNIQUE (D) gives you a series of questionable questions to think about and provides you an opportunity to formulate your own response.

RESPONSE TECHNIQUE D:
Questionable Questions — General

QUESTION #1:   *"When were you born?"*

or

"How old are you?"

or

"What is your birthday — month, day, and year?"
(or any other question that indicates your age)

Poor Response: "It is illegal to ask that question and I refuse to answer."

GOOD Response: "I am mature enough to be responsible but young enough to be flexible."

KEY CONCEPT

This response will help you avoid the issue of age while illustrating your positive attitude.

Your Response: _____

_____

_____

_____

_____

_____

QUESTION #2:   *"What does your spouse do for a living?"*

Poor Response: "He is a plumber."

                              or

                 "That is none of your business."

GOOD Response: "I am not sure if I understand how the answer to that question is relevant to job performance or qualifications."

KEY CONCEPT

Questions referring to your marital status should not be asked. If asked, relate your concern about the importance of that question . . . relative to the job. Answer in a manner that will shift the burden back to the interviewer.

Your Response:_____

_____

_____

_____

_____

_____

_____

QUESTION #3:   *"Tell me about your family."*

Poor Response: "I have three children of preschool
                   age. They are really great and I en-
                   joy them . . ."

GOOD Response: "I have no family problems that will
                   interfere with job performance."

KEY CONCEPT

Avoid talking about your family or financial need. If you are a woman with children, many prospective employers will doubt your ability to get to work on time. Always refer to your excellent performance in your response.

Your Response:_____

_____

_____

_____

_____

_____

_____

_____

QUESTION #4:   *"Do you have any physical or mental problems?"*

Poor Response: "I have a bad back, am blind in one eye, and can't see out of the other."

GOOD Response: "I am probably like most human beings and have some minor limitations, but if you describe the requirements of the job, I will relate my assets and limitations relative to those requirements."

KEY CONCEPT

All people have limitations and handicaps. Do not start telling all of your limitations UNLESS they will interfere with your job performance. If your hands are allergic to chicken fat, a restaurant owner should be made aware of the problem whereas that information is not necessary for a typing job.

Your Response:_____

_____

_____

_____

_____

SPECIAL TECHNIQUES
FOR THE EX-OFFENDER

Employers are usually concerned about individuals who have felony records . . . that is, individuals who have been convicted of a felony (serious crime).

Misdemeanors (minor crime violations such as speeding, disorderly conduct, etc.) are usually not the object of the interviewer's questions. If the job you are interviewing for relates directly to a misdemeanor conviction, it is best to discuss it in the interview. (EXAMPLE: An applicant with two counts of drunk driving in one year applying for a job as a taxi cab driver.) All other misdemeanor discussion can be avoided.

The following section is a brief but relevant description of how to handle serious crime questions for the ex-offender.

QUESTION #5:   *"Have you ever been arrested?"*

Poor Response: "I have been arrested for speeding and narcotics violations."

GOOD Response: "I have never been convicted of any serious crime."

KEY CONCEPT

Employers should ask only about convictions, not arrests. Unless you are applying for a job that requires a driving license, traffic violations need not be mentioned. If you are applying for a driving job, respond to the traffic violation question only when asked.

Your Response:_____

_____

_____

_____

_____

_____

_____

QUESTION #6:   *"Have you ever been convicted of a crime?"*

If you have NEVER been convicted, simply answer, "No, I have not."

If you have been convicted of a crime, the following information should be considered carefully.

OPTION #1

Poor Response: "I have been convicted of writing bad checks and interstate transportation of stolen goods."

GOOD Response: "If we could take just a minute, I would like to share a problem that I encountered in the past. I was young and foolish and went for a joy ride several years ago. I crossed the state line in a car that was not mine. I was with a group of young people . . . and well, you know how it is. If we had not crossed the state line, I would have had no serious problems. I want to tell you here and now that I really learned from that experience. I have been sorry for my involvement ever since."

NEVER SAY: "armed robbery" —
DO SAY: "took something that was not mine."

NEVER SAY: "car theft" —
DO SAY: "took a car that did not belong to me for
              a ride."

NEVER SAY: "narcotics conviction" —
DO SAY: "had a legal problem with drugs in the
              past and have learned from it."

Always use mild, indirect terms instead of the harsh, direct term for the crime. If you have had several convictions, do not volunteer information . . . mention the least serious crime. If the interviewer is satisfied with your first conviction reaction, questions about other arrests may not even come up.

KEY CONCEPT

 Admit your mistake, be repentant, and show that you learned from the experience.

Your Response:_____

_____

_____

_____

_____

_____

OPTION #2

If you have been convicted of a crime you can always just avoid the truth . . . that is, lie about your conviction(s) to the interviewer. Be sure, however, if you go this route that you are an expert liar because most employers hire on the basis of information available and gut level feelings. Most interviewers are good at recognizing inconsistencies in discussions and body language clues.

KEY CONCEPT

 THIS OPTION IS NOT GENERALLY RECOMMENDED. Even if you get the job, you must continue to live the lie during the entire employment period with the company because you can be fired for lying during the application process. You can be fired at ANY stage of employment.

Your Response:_____
_____
_____
_____
_____
_____
_____

SUMMARY

Temper your answers with wisdom. Be cooperative and be sure the interviewer knows you are putting out your best effort so that employment decisions can be made. You are also interviewing that company to see if you really want to work there. If the interviewer appears to try to run you over by asking illegal questions or by executive power, you may have second thoughts. You will discover that looking for a job is similar to buying a suit of clothes or a used car . . . you must know what suits your needs and then shop around until you find WHAT YOU WANT!

An applicant who strictly interprets the law during the interview and refuses to answer questions will probably not be hired because inflexibility is implied. An applicant who can "skirt" a confrontation issue and still answer the question can probably get along in many situations. This type of individual has employment potential and will be hired.

CHAPTER 5

Employment Applications

TALE OF WOE

APPLICATION INFORMATION TOOL

Employment Applications

TALE OF WOE

(Picture the following:)

Mickey, a job-seeker, enters the employment office of a large company and requests an employment application. With a blank expression, she accepts the form, fumbles in her purse and realizes she did not bring a pencil or pen. The secretary hands her a "company" pencil (one so short, thick, and dull that no one could print between the application form lines). As Mickey begins to fill out the form she enters her name and address in good fashion . . . but what is her social security number? As she empties the contents of her purse, she realizes her social security card is at home in her jewelry box and she can't remember the number. Mickey takes a guess . . . after all, the company wouldn't know if it is really her number or not.

Application Form: EDUCATION

Mickey cannot recall the year she graduated or how to spell the name of the high school. Mickey's uncertainty level rises with the forgotten dates and spelling.

Application Form: EMPLOYMENT HISTORY

Why do they always want the company name AND address? Mickey asks the secretary for a telephone book . . . she just can't seem to remember when she worked there . . . was it June, 1984 or July, 1985? Oh, no! Someone has torn out the page she needed in the telephone book . . . and why do company pencils all seem to have the erasers chewed off! Will anyone notice the hole she has made with the almost non-existent eraser . . . or the sweat . . . or the tears?

(It has been over an hour since Mickey began filling out the employment application.)

Application Form: REFERENCES

Mickey crumbles up the employment application and runs out of the office . . . screaming!

This story of woe is not uncommon. Some people take hours to fill out an employment application. This is not necessary since most companies require similar information and/or have identical employment applications. Therefore, if you gather your personal information BEFOREHAND, all you have to do is copy it onto the employment application. The APPLICATION INFOR-MATION TOOL will be your key to low frustration job application processing. It will enable you to fill out employment applications in about seven minutes, there-by avoiding Mickey's tale of woe.

An example of the APPLICATION INFORMA-TION TOOL has been filled in for your reference start-ing on page 81.

A blank copy of the APPLICATION INFORMA-TION TOOL is provided at the end of the book, starting on page 245.

As you fill out your APPLICATION INFORMA-TION TOOL, use the following pages as a guide.

APPLICATION INFORMATION TOOL

Instructions: Fill in the blank APPLICATION INFOR-
MATION TOOL (at the end of this book, page 245)
based on the following recommendations. Do your
RESEARCH NOW . . . not later.

NAME: __**MOORE**_____**MICKEY**_____**M**_____
        (Last)   (First)   (Middle)

NAME: Unless the application directs you to write,
PRINT your last name in BOLD print so that it stands
out and is easy for the interviewer to see and remember.

NAME: __MOORE_____MICKEY_____M_____
        (Last)   (First)   (Middle)

ADDRESS: __123 BAY DR SAN DIEGO, CA 92010__
          (Street)   (City)   (State)   (Zip)

ADDRESS: PRINT your address making sure all is
correct. Know your ZIP CODE and include it!

NAME: _MOORE_____MICKEY_____M_____
       (Last)   (First)   (Middle)

ADDRESS: _123_BAY_DR___SAN DIEGO, CA___92010_
       (Street)   (City) (State) (Zip)

PHONE NUMBER: (714)___222-1022_____
       (714)___222-1198_____
           (Message Number)

PHONE NUMBER: List your phone number and/or the phone number of a person who can take a message for you (a relative, friend, or landlord who is usually at home). You may not be home to respond to a job offer.

NAME: _MOORE,_____MICKEY_____M_____
       (Last)   (First)   (Middle)

ADDRESS: _123_BAY_DR_SAN DIEGO_CA_92010_
       (Street)   (City) (State) (Zip)

PHONE NUMBER: (714)___222-1022_____
       (714)___222-1198_____
           (Message Number)

SOCIAL SECURITY NUMBER: **580-40-1222**

DRIVER'S LICENSE NUMBER: _S082481_____

SOCIAL SECURITY NUMBER:
DRIVER'S LICENSE NUMBER: Number sequences are easy to forget so WRITE THEM DOWN!

NAME: __MOORE_____MICKEY_____M____
      (Last)   (First)   (Middle)

ADDRESS: _123__BAY__DR___SAN_DIEGO__CA_92010_
       (Street)   (City)   (State)   (Zip)

PHONE NUMBER: _(714)___222-1022_____
            _(714)___222-1198_____
                (Message Number)

SOCIAL SECURITY NUMBER: _580-40-1222_____

DRIVER'S LICENSE NUMBER: __SO82481_____

EDUCATION:

Grade School	Years Attended	Degree
ADAMS	8	DIPLOMA
LINCOLN, INDIANA		

EDUCATION — GRADE SCHOOL: All you need to do is indicate the number of years attended. If you write down the dates, it is a clue to your age. The word diploma shows that you have graduated.

NAME: _MOORE_____MICKEY_____M_____
          (Last)   (First)   (Middle)

ADDRESS: _123 BAY DR SAN DIEGO CA 92010_
         (Street)   (City)   (State)   (Zip)

PHONE NUMBER: _(714) 222-1022_____
             _(714) 222-1198_____
             (Message Number)

SOCIAL SECURITY NUMBER: _580-40-1222_____

·DRIVER'S LICENSE NUMBER: _SO82481_____

EDUCATION:

Grade School	Years Attended	Degree
ADAMS	8	DIPLOMA
LINCOLN, INDIANA		

High School	Years Attended	Degree
MUTUAL HIGH SCHOOL	4	DIPLOMA
NATIONAL CITY, CA		

EDUCATION — HIGH SCHOOL: You should identify only the high school last attended or graduated from. If you have a diploma equivalency in the form of a General Education Development (G.E.D.), General Adult Diploma, or have passed a high school proficiency test, write that instead of the word diploma. If you did not graduate or attain an equivalency, write in the highest grade completed.

Remember . . . federal law prohibits a high school from releasing any information about you (other than the fact that you may have attended) to anyone without your written permission.

NAME: __MOORE_____MICKEY_____M_____
        (Last)   (First)   (Middle)
ADDRESS: 123 BAY DR   SAN DIEGO CA 92010
          (Street)   (City)   (State)   (Zip)
PHONE NUMBER: (714) 222-1022
              (714) 222-1198
                   (Message Number)
SOCIAL SECURITY NUMBER: 580-40-1222
DRIVER'S LICENSE NUMBER: S082481
EDUCATION:

Grade School	Years Attended	Degree
ADAMS	8	DIPLOMA
LINCOLN, INDIANA		

High School	Years Attended	Degree
MUTUAL HIGH SCHOOL	4	DIPLOMA
NATIONAL CITY, CA		

College	Years Attended	Degree
HILLTOP COLLEGE	1963	24 UNITS
SAN DIEGO, CA		GENERAL EDUCATION
		BUSINESS COURSES

EDUCATION — COLLEGE: Record the major colleges attended. If the space on the actual application is limited, identify those colleges from which you have graduated and/or taken classes that are applicable to the job for which you are applying.

NAME: __MOORE_____MICKEY_____M____
       (Last)   (First)   (Middle)

ADDRESS: _123 BAY DR SAN DIEGO CA 92010_
        (Street)   (City)   (State)   (Zip)

PHONE NUMBER: __(714)__222-1222_____
           (714)__222-1198_____
               (Message Number)

SOCIAL SECURITY NUMBER: _580-40-1222_

DRIVER'S LICENSE NUMBER: _S082481_____

EDUCATION:

Grade School	Years Attended	Degree
ADAMS	8	DIPLOMA
LINCOLN, INDIANA		

High School	Years Attended	Degree
MUTUAL HIGH SCHOOL	4	DIPLOMA
NATIONAL CITY, CA		

College	Years Attended	Degree
HILLTOP COLLEGE	1963	24 UNITS
		GENERAL EDUCATION
		BUSINESS COURSES

Trade, Business, Correspondence:	Years Attended:	Degree:
VELA SECRETARIAL COLLEGE	1965	CERTIFICATE

(GENERAL OFFICE - TYPING, BOOKKEEPING, FILING, DICTAPHONE, TRANSCRIPTION)

EDUCATION — TRADE, BUSINESS, CORRE-SPONDENCE: This category can include public, private, military, and/or mail order schools. This category will be a strong selling point for many jobs. A company would rather hire a person who has learned secretarial skills at a business school than a college graduate with little or no training for a secretarial position.

EDUCATION:

Grade School	Years Attended	Degree
ADAMS	8	DIPLOMA
LINCOLN, INDIANA		

High School	Years Attended	Degree
MUTUAL HIGH SCHOOL.	4	DIPLOMA
NATIONAL CITY, CA		

College	Years Attended	Degree
HILLTOP COLLEGE	1963	24 UNITS
		GENERAL EDUCATION
		BUSINESS COURSES

Trade, Business, Correspondence	Years Attended	Degree
VELA SECRETARIAL COLLEGE	1965	
(GENERAL OFFICE - TYPING, BOOKKEEPING		
FILING, DICTAPHONE, TRANSCRIPTION)		

Special Study, Research, Apprenticeships, On-the-job training
PERSONNEL HIRING SEMINAR -
ABC COMPANY, 1971
UNITED STATES NAVY- YEOMAN CLASS 'A'
SCHOOL · SAN DIEGO, CA 1966

EDUCATION — SPECIAL STUDY, RESEARCH,
APPRENTICESHIPS, ON-THE-JOB TRAINING:
Any special training that falls under this broad
category should be mentioned if the real application
asks for it. If you have experienced many inservice
training programs, select those that are most impressive. Do not attempt to write all of them down on the
application. Many can be listed on your resume (to be
discussed in Chapter 9).

OPTION #1 — Paid Work Experience

EMPLOYMENT HISTORY:

Company Name: *ABC COMPANY*

Address: *18140 UNION BOULEVARD, S.D. CA 92111*

Position: *PERSONNEL DEPARTMENT CLERK*

Duties: *TYPING, INCOMING MAIL, EMPLOYMENT SCREENING & PROCESSING*

Supervisor: *MS ANNE BOYD* Title: *PERSONNEL MGR*

Starting Date: *SEPTEMBER 28, 1971*

Termination Date: *PRESENTLY EMPLOYED*

Reason for Leaving: *BETTER SALARY· JOB ADVANCEMENT*

Hourly Wage: *$ 4.50*

EMPLOYMENT HISTORY: This section of the application is for PAID WORK EXPERIENCE only. Always print out the entire company name and address. The position you held should be in standard wording such as truck driver (not long hauler) or police officer (not cop).

Describe the duties briefly and specifically. You will be able to elaborate during the interview.

Spelling of the supervisor's name and title should be correct.

The start date and termination date need only be approximate. Jobs shorter than one or two months probably should not be mentioned. A few weeks gap (periods of non-work) are not too problematic on your application. The important factor here is to have your application show you have experience relative to the given job.

OPTION #2 — Volunteer Experience

EMPLOYMENT HISTORY:

Company Name: **NATIONAL LITTLE LEAGUE ASSN.**
Address: **10281 MASK SANTEE, CA 92071**
Position: **ADVERTISING & PROMOTION DIRECTOR**
Duties: **PUBLIC RELATIONS, PRESS RELEASES,
MEMBERSHIP**
Supervisor: **MR. BRIAN CLARK**   Title: **STATE MANAGER**
Starting Date: **DECEMBER, 1968**
Termination Date: **DECEMBER, 1970**
Reason for Leaving: **FULL TIME EMPLOYMENT**
Hourly Wage: **VOLUNTEER**

EMPLOYMENT HISTORY: You may have both paid and unpaid (volunteer) experience listed on the application. Volunteer (unpaid) work is valid employment experience if related to the job for which you are applying. Handle volunteer work like paid work experience (previously discussed). Provide the requested information but put the word "volunteer" where "Hourly Wage" is indicated.

Remember to list volunteer experience on your resume (to be discussed in Chapter 9). A volunteer resume example is provided on page 218.

OPTION #3 — No Paid or Volunteer Experience

EMPLOYMENT HISTORY:

Company Name: _____

Address: _____

Position: _____

Duties: _____

_____

Supervisor: _____ Title: _____

Starting Date: _____

Termination Date: _____

Reason for Leaving: _____

Hourly Wage: _____

WILL BE DISCUSSED DURING THE INTERVIEW

EMPLOYMENT HISTORY: If you have no paid or volunteer work experience, put a slash through the lines on the application and print, "WILL BE DISCUSSED DURING THE INTERVIEW."

MILITARY SERVICE:

Branch: __USN_____ Dates: 1·10·66 – 12·18·70

Rate/Rank Upon Discharge: PETTY OFFICER 3RD CLASS (E4)

Job Description: YEOMAN : CLERICAL

Discharge: HONORABLE

MILITARY SERVICE: If you did serve in the military, you can abbreviate the title: USN (United States Navy), USMC (United States Marine Corps), USAF (United States Air Force), USA (United States Army), USCG (United States Coast Guard), or USNG (United States National Guard). An -R suffix to any of the abbreviations indicates "Reserve" (example: USN-R means United States Navy-Reserve).

Print the starting and ending dates of active service only.

Print the correct title of your military job as space is available.

Indicate type of military discharge.

MILITARY SERVICE:

Branch: _USN_____ Dates: _1·10·66 – 12·18·70_

Rate/Rank Upon Discharge: _PETTY OFFICER 3RD CLASS (E4)_

Job Description: _YEOMAN · CLERICAL_____

Discharge: _HONORABLE_____

JOB YOU ARE APPLYING FOR:

EXECUTIVE SECRETARY

JOB YOU ARE APPLYING FOR: Do some research on the company to find out about their products or needs. You might even ask the receptionist about the company as you come in to fill out the employment application.

Have a specific job in mind that you are applying for even though you may take an alternate job just to get into the company. A person who is willing to do anything usually ends up with nothing. Having specific skills is an insurance policy for getting a specific job. If the company thinks they want you (as a person), they may offer you an alternative job until the job you applied for opens up.

MILITARY SERVICE:

    Branch: _USN_   Dates: _1·10·66 - 12·18·70_

    Rate/Rank Upon Discharge: _PETTY OFFICER 3RD CLASS (E4)_

    Job Description: _YEOMAN : CLERICAL_

    Discharge: _HONORABLE_

JOB YOU ARE APPLYING FOR:

    EXECUTIVE SECRETARY

ANTICIPATED SALARY:

                 OPEN

ANTICIPATED SALARY: If you know the going rate of pay for the kind of work you do, print in the hourly rate or weekly/monthly salary. You should be sure, however, that if you print in an amount that is the going rate and later find you have sold yourself too low, it is difficult, if not impossible, to negotiate a higher amount after you are hired. Then again, if you are 50% too high, the company may not even talk to you.

The word OPEN is what to print if you are not too sure of the going rate for the job.

MILITARY SERVICE:

Branch: _USN_   Dates: _1·10·66– 12·18·70_

Rate/Rank Upon Discharge: _PETTY OFFICER 3RD CLASS (E4)_

Job Description: _YEOMAN : CLERICAL_

Discharge: _HONORABLE_

JOB YOU ARE APPLYING FOR:

EXECUTIVE SECRETARY

ANTICIPATED SALARY:

OPEN

PROFESSIONAL ORGANIZATIONS:

NATIONAL SECRETARIES ASSN/TOASTMASTERS

PROFESSIONAL ORGANIZATIONS: Print any professional organizations you belong to that would imply favorable employment potential.

REFERENCES: **LIEUTENANT COMMANDER PAUL STONE**
Name
PERSONNEL OFFICER
Title
UNITED STATES NAVY
Company Name
442 MARINE WAY
Address
SAN DIEGO   CA   92010
City   State   Zip
714   560·8441
Area Code   Telephone Number

DR. ARNOLD BYE
Name
RESEARCH SPECIALIST
Title
ATOMIC DESIGN
Company Name
8100 `B' STREET
Address
NATIONAL CITY   CA   92011
City   State   Zip
714   443-8200
Area Code   Telephone Number

MRS JACKIE JACKSON
Name
VICE PRESIDENT
Title
ABC COMPANY
Company Name
18140 UNION BLVD
Address
SAN DIEGO,   CA   92111
City   State   Zip
714   561-8993
Area Code   Telephone Number

REFERENCES: If you have work experience, work references are best to give.

If you have little work experience, then give personal references (reliable people who know you).

ALWAYS ask your potential references for permission to use their names.

Use correct introductory titles (Mr., Mrs., Ms., Dr.). List business addresses and phone numbers where references can be reached during working hours.

Be specific and correct with the occupational job title of your reference.

SUMMARY

Remember to always carry two sharp pencils with erasers, a pen with erasable-type ink, and a completed APPLICATION INFORMATION TOOL. The faster you fill out employment applications, the more places you visit . . . and, the more chances you have of finding employment.

Be sure to fill in all blanks on the application form. Print NA (meaning not applicable) where the information requested does not apply to you.

It is illegal to ask questions about your age, sex,
marital status, national origin, or race on an application
form. However, many companies still request that information. If you fill out an application form and desire not
to answer those questions, print WILL DISCUSS IN
INTERVIEW (see Chapter 4 entitled QUESTION-
ABLE QUESTIONS). Most employers are not aware of
the law and do not mean personal harm by having those
questions on the application form. If it is not detrimen-
tal to your employment potential, it is suggested that
you show your flexibility by answering the questions.

Now that you have labored through this APPLI-
CATION INFORMATION TOOL . . .

NEVER THROW IT AWAY!!!

Update this valuable TOOL as need be. It contains
all the information you will need when applying for a
job. Now you can just copy your information onto the
employment application form . . . and do it in about
seven minutes!

APPLICATION INFORMATION TOOL

NAME: **MOORE**   MICKEY   M
      (Last)   (First)   (Middle)

ADDRESS: 123 BAY DR   SAN DIEGO, CA   92010
      (Street)   (City)   (State)   (Zip)

PHONE NUMBER: (714) 222-1022

                (714) 222-1198
                     (Message Number)

SOCIAL SECURITY NUMBER: 580-40-1222

DRIVER'S LICENSE NUMBER: S082481

EDUCATION:

Grade School:	Years Attended:	Degree:
ADAMS	8	DIPLOMA
LINCOLN, INDIANA		

High School	Years Attended:	Degree:
MUTUAL HIGH SCHOOL	4	DIPLOMA
NATIONAL CITY, CA		

College:	Years Attended:	Degree:
HILLTOP COLLEGE	1963	24 UNITS
SAN DIEGO, CA		GENERAL EDUCATION
		BUSINESS COURSES

Trade, Business, Correspondence: Years Attended: Degree:

VELA SECRETARIAL COLLEGE 1965
(GENERAL OFFICE - TYPING, BOOKKEEPING
FILING, DICTAPHONE TRANSCRIPTION)

Special Study, Research, Apprenticeships, On-the-job training:

PERSONNEL HIRING SEMINAR —
ABC COMPANY 1971,
UNITED STATES NAVY · YEOMAN CLASS 'A'
SCHOOL - SAN DIEGO CA 10.71

APPLICATION INFORMATION TOOL — Continued

EMPLOYMENT HISTORY:

Company Name: _ABC COMPANY_

Address: _18140 UNION BOULEVARD S.D CA 92111_

Position: _PERSONNEL DEPARTMENT CLERK_

Duties: _TYPING, INCOMING MAIL, EMPLOYMENT SCREENING & PROCESSING_

Supervisor: _MS ANNE BOYD_   Title: _PERSONNEL MGR_

Starting Date: _SEPTEMBER 28, 1971_

Termination Date: _PRESENTLY EMPLOYED_

Reason for Leaving: _BETTER SALARY-JOB ADVANCEMENT_

Hourly Wage: _$4.50_

Company Name: _KAISER COMPANY_

Address: _281 FOURTH AVENUE S.D. CA 92103_

Position: _SECRETARY_

Duties: _ANSWERING INQUIRIES, DICTAPHONE GENERAL OFFICE_

Supervisor: _MRS BETTY JAY_ Title: _OFFICE MANAGER_

Starting Date: _APRIL 12, 1970_

Termination Date: _SEPTEMBER 25, 1971_

Reason for Leaving: _BETTER SALARY_

Hourly Wage: _$3.75_

Company Name: _MILLER CONSTRUCTION_

Address: _22400 DIVISION AVE NATL CTY CA 42408_

Position: _SECRETARY_

Duties: _TELEPHONE, TYPING, FILING_

Supervisor: _MR BILL MILLER_ Title: _PRESIDENT_

Starting Date: _DECEMBER 28, 1970_

Termination Date: _APRIL 10, 1971_

Reason for Leaving: _COMPANY WENT OUT OF BUSINESS_

Hourly Wage: _$3.50_

APPLICATION INFORMATION TOOL — Continued

MILITARY SERVICE:

Branch: _USN_   Dates: _1·10·66 — 12·18·70_

Rate/Rank Upon Discharge: _PETTY OFFICER 3RD CLASS (E4)_

Job Description: _YEOMAN : CLERICAL_

Discharge: _HONORABLE_

JOB YOU ARE APPLYING FOR:

EXECUTIVE SECRETARY

ANTICIPATED SALARY:

OPEN

PROFESSIONAL ORGANIZATIONS:

NATIONAL SECRETARIES ASSN / TOASTMASTERS

REFERENCES: _LIEUTENANT COMMANDER PAUL STONE_
Name

PERSONNEL OFFICER
Title

UNITED STATES NAVY
Company Name

442 MARINE WAY
Address

SAN DIEGO,   _CA_   _92010_
City   State   Zip

_714_   _560 - 8441_
Area Code   Telephone Number

DR ARNOLD BYE
Name
RESEARCH SPECIALIST
Title
ATOMIC DESIGN
Company Name
8100 'B' STREET
Address
NATIONAL CITY,   CA   92011
City   State   Zip
714   443-8200
Area Code   Telephone Number

MRS. JACKIE JACKSON
Name
VICE PRESIDENT
Title
ABC COMPANY
Company Name
18140 UNION BOULEVARD
Address
SAN DIEGO,   CA   9211
City   State   Zip
714   561-8993
Area Code   Telephone Number

CHAPTER 6

Employment Openings

PLACES TO LOOK

POUNDING THE PAVEMENT TECHNIQUE

POUNDING THE PAVEMENT TOOL

LET YOUR FINGERS DO THE WALKING
TECHNIQUE

LET YOUR FINGERS DO THE WALKING
DRAMATIZATION

PHONE SEARCH TOOL

PHONE SCRIPT TOOL

INTERVIEW INFORMATION TOOL

Employment Openings

PLACES TO LOOK

Knowing where to find an employment opening is as important as knowing how to work. Many people learn a skill only to be frustrated when they cannot find a suitable opportunity (job opening) to practice that skill.

Where are the good jobs? How are they found? Where does one begin? This chapter will answer these questions.

Recently a large metropolitan area firm ran a classified advertisement for twenty training positions to which over one thousand applicants responded. Remember . . . only about 5% (five out of 100) of all jobs available are advertised in the newspaper and many applicants will apply, thus making the competition for that particular job very keen indeed!

Finding employment openings is not mystical, magical, or accidental. Purposeful and directive effort is the key to success. Looking for a job is like fishing . . . the more hooks you have on the line, the better the chance of catching a fish. The more places you apply, the better opportunity you have for job procurement. If you never get your line wet, you will never land the BIG one.

The following is a comprehensive list of places
where you can find employment openings. They are
given in order of potential success for job attainment,
but do not overlook any of the suggestions because any
one of them could be your key to employment.

FIRST PLACE: Friends, Relatives, Neighbors;
                    Networking

Enlist the aid of your friends, relatives, and neighbors to inform you of job openings. This approach to
finding employment is commonly called "Networking."
Many companies hire from the inside . . . that is, they
ask their trusted employees if they know of anyone who
might be looking for a job. Many jobs are filled before
the general public even discovers that there was an
opening. Inform everyone you know that you are looking for work and a good job lead may materialize. [If you
have a resume (see Chapter 9), distribute it freely to all
your friends, relatives, and neighbors.]

SECOND PLACE: Personnel and Employment Offices

Apply at the personnel or employment offices of
both large and small businesses. The next section of this
Chapter, POUNDING THE PAVEMENT TECH-
NIQUE, will give you detailed information regarding
successful utilization of this effective way of finding
employment openings.

THIRD PLACE: Telephone Book

Use the telephone to find employment openings and arrange for interviews. The LET YOUR FINGERS DO THE WALKING TECHNIQUE section of this chapter will give a comprehensive explanation of how to successfully utilize this effective way of finding employment openings.

FOURTH PLACE: Chamber of Commerce

Use your local Chamber of Commerce's *Business Directory* for information about local industries and places of employment. The Chamber of Commerce may even assist you with a job lead.

FIFTH PLACE: Church

Elicit information from church membership and/or church leaders. Many activities revolving around a church can give you a job lead. Some churches have membership and/or service lists that can aid you. A discussion with the pastor or participation in a church activity can develop job leads.

SIXTH PLACE: Employment Development Department

Check with your local Employment Development Department (E.D.D.) office, where a variety of employment services are available. This is a no-fee state government agency assisting individuals with unemployment benefits, job placement, vocational testing (some locations), and other job-related services. They also have a job placement service based on requests made by employers. Call the telephone directory information operator for the telephone number and location nearest you.

SEVENTH PLACE: Schools

Check with your school, community college, or university placement office. Many schools are contacted by employers looking for suitable employees. This can include local high schools (regular and adult), private schools, and post secondary schools.

EIGHTH PLACE: Government

Investigate federal, state, county, and city personnel offices for job leads. Since each branch of government has its own procedures for employment application, it is best to call the particular branch you may be interested in working for to attain information. Each particular branch of government is listed differently according to various telephone books, but the following is the general way government agencies are listed:

CITY: Look under the city by name . . . then under Employment or Personnel.

COUNTY: Look under the county by name . . . then under Employment or Personnel.

STATE: Look under the state by name . . . then under Employment Development Department.

FEDERAL: Look under United States Government . . . then under Federal Job Information Center.

If you cannot find these listings, call the telephone directory information operator for the correct phone number.

NINTH PLACE: Newspaper

Check the classified ads as listed in your local newspaper. Keep in mind, however, the following regarding newspaper advertisements:

1. Only about 5% (five out of 100) available jobs are listed in the newspaper.
2. Competition is keen. As many as 40 or 50 qualified people may apply for that same advertised position.
3. Sometimes companies with government contracts are required by law to officially advertise openings while the vacancy is already unofficially filled.

TENTH PLACE: Unions

Check local labor unions for openings in their particular craft or trade. Generally, labor unions control employment in specific trades rather than employing individuals. If you are interested in a specific trade (or have experience in one), approach the local union hall regarding employment opportunities.

ELEVENTH PLACE: Private Agencies

Private employment agencies, sometimes called placement agencies, are available to help you find a job. You literally pay these agencies to look for you. The cost can be as high as a month's salary, even if you lose the job. Some private agency fees are paid by the employers, but you should be well aware of your financial obligations BEFORE signing any contract.

MISCELLANEOUS

TEMPORARY or CASUAL LABOR MARKET

If you need immediate employment (either on a part-time or full-time basis), and must be paid daily, you should investigate the temporary or casual labor market.

Services listed under "Employment: Temporary" in the Yellow Pages of your telephone book utilize people on a daily basis. The temporary service has you on call and is in contact with local industry. When industry needs an individual temporarily, the company calls the service who in turn calls you for work. There is usually no charge to you for this service and you can usually be paid on a daily basis.

Temporary or casual employment can lead to full-time employment if you are a productive person. This may be an option for you if you are re-entering the labor market after inactive years. This allows you to ease back into the labor market and get used to a full day of work.

OUT-OF-TOWN OPPORTUNITIES

You may want to seek employment in a city that is not close to your current residence. You may want to go 100 miles or 1,000 miles. If you carefully develop job search strategies you can be successfully employed, have a good place to live, and make the move with little or no lost income.

Job-seeking for out-of-town opportunities takes some planning and research but can be accomplished. The following are TECHNIQUES that will work for you:

1. Ask friends and relatives who live in the desired city to send you information regarding employment opportunities. This can be clippings from the classified sections of various newspapers, last year's copy of the Yellow Pages, or their knowledge of specific job openings.

2. Order a one- to three-months subscription to the out-of-town newspaper and have it mailed to your home. This is not only a clue to job openings but can give you information regarding cost of living (rent, house prices, food, etc.) and weather conditions.

3. Many libraries have Yellow Pages for cities in other areas of the United States. This can supply you with company names and addresses where letters of application and copies of your resume can be sent.

4. You can contact the Chamber of Commerce and purchase a copy of their *Business Directory* listing most local companies. The cost is from $5 to $20 and will render valuable data about local company names, size, what they produce or provide, and the names of the various officers.

5. You can contact out-of-town companies by calling long distance. Your chances for success will be greatly improved if you use the technique described on page 107, LET YOUR FINGERS DO THE WALKING, as a general guideline. Make sure any commitment made can be kept; i.e., interview date and time.

6. Libraries usually carry many employment-related reference materials that can be useful in your job search. Examples are the *Thomas Register* or *Contacts Influential* which list specific industries and services by city. These are cross-references to specific company descriptions, sizes, names and addresses of officers.

7. You can take a vacation or business trip to the city
    you are interested in before making a permanent
    commitment. You can make a more data-based de-
    cision if you have visited both industrial and tourist
    areas in a city.

8. You may want to "trial work" a job before moving
    your belongings (family, clothes, furniture, etc.) to a
    new location. You can take personal leave time from
    your current job, move to the destination you
    desire, rent an apartment or buy or rent a small
    trailer, and "trial work" the job. If, after a couple of
    months there is still promise, you can relocate your
    belongings with relative security.

KEY CONCEPT

Employers are seeking good employees. It is your job to find them and make them aware of YOU. Use any or all of the places listed for seeking employment openings. Do not give up and your job search will be successful.

Keep in mind the temporary or casual labor market as an effective way to earn quick money and which could lead to full-time employment.

When looking for employment opportunities out-of-town, collect job-related information via friends, relatives, newspapers, business directories, or organize a vacation to where you want to work. Send a letter of application and a resume to the companies that appeal to you. Avoid moving your belongings until you have "trial worked" a job or at least have been given written assurance of a position.

Now that you have seen where to look for employment, the next sections will expand on two of these places . . . EMPLOYMENT OFFICES (POUNDING THE PAVEMENT TECHNIQUE and TOOL) and the TELEPHONE BOOK (LET YOUR FINGERS DO THE WALKING TECHNIQUE and related TOOLS).

POUNDING THE PAVEMENT TECHNIQUE

Pounding the pavement is taking the opportunity to seek employment by going from company to company in person. This takes much energy but is quite productive in gaining successful employment. Being aggressive enough to fill out applications without complaint is often admired by potential employers who may hire you on the spot. Other employers, however, will not even take a resume or application. It is like the slot machines in Las Vegas . . . pay the money and take your chances.

The morning is generally the best time to go job seeking. Personnel managers are usually fresh and can give you a good interview from 8:30 a.m. to 11:00 a.m. As the lunch period approaches the chances of a poor interview increase. The interviewer is no different from the person being interviewed . . . hunger, or any other body discomfort, tends to cause an unfavorable mental outlook.

Treat yourself to a good lunch (even if it stretches your budget) because job-seeking takes tremendous effort and will drain your physical reserves.

You can look for work from 1:00 p.m. to 3:30 p.m., but be aware of your own feelings and physical condition. When you are freshly invigorated, turn downs are acceptable. If you have experienced several morning turn downs you may come across poorly in an afternoon interview. It may be better to approach the company the next morning.

Persistence is your KEY to employment. For every ten visits you should have one to three interviews. It is not uncommon to visit 60 to 80 companies (six to 10 job-seeking days) before finding satisfactory employment. Also, it is not uncommon to have two to three job offers on the same day. Continue to visit personnel offices until you get the job you want.

Avoid feelings of persecution. Job-seeking can be emotionally distressing. Remember . . . employers are looking for suitable employees and prospective employees are looking for suitable employment. Getting the two together is a sometimes difficult but not impossible task.

Make sure to bring along your APPLICATION IN-FORMATION TOOL (Chapter 5) to copy your information onto the company employment application, as well as a pencil and an erasable ballpoint pen.

Now, as you enter the employment offices of these companies, develop a script along the following guidelines:

Receptionist: "Good morning! Can I help you?"
JOB-SEEKER: "Good morning. I have skills as a
                 _____." (secretary,
                 welder, mechanic, etc. . . . whatever
                 your skills are.) "Does your company
                 ever hire in skill areas similar to
                 mine?"

The following are three possible responses you may receive and the way to deal with each:

POSSIBLE RESPONSE #1:

Receptionist: "We do have an opening. Would you
                 fill out an application, please.
                 Do you have time for an interview
                 today?"
JOB-SEEKER: "Yes, I would be happy to interview.
                 Thank you."

POSSIBLE RESPONSE #2:

Receptionist:	"If you will have a seat, I will check to see if we can use you."
JOB-SEEKER:	"Thank you. Would you like a copy of my resume?"
Receptionist:	(as she turns to go into another office) "Yes, thank you." (after an inter-office conference) "We have no openings at this time."
JOB-SEEKER:	"May I fill out an application or leave my resume?"
Receptionist:	"Yes, please fill out an application and attach your resume."

HINT: If she says "No, we are not taking applications," you can be reasonably sure there are no openings and can leave knowing you have done everything you could to apply for a job.

POSSIBLE RESPONSE #3:

Receptionist: "We have no openings and are not
                 accepting applications."
JOB-SEEKER: "I understand, but, before I leave . . .
                 for my own records . . . who is the
                 person in charge of hiring?"
Receptionist: "Mr. Brown, but he is not seeing
                 anyone."
JOB-SEEKER: "Thank you for your time . . . and
                 have a good day."

   HINT: The receptionist is probably correct in
           the statement that the company is
           not hiring . . . but, if you can get the
           name of the person who is responsible,
           you can call him later by phone.

           AVOID irritating the reception-
           ist. Give receptionists your highest
           regard for they hold your destiny in
           their hands. They can indicate your
           attitude to the interviewer before you
           even have the chance to impress him
           or her.

KEY CONCEPT

As a job-seeker you should concentrate your efforts on making good impressions and collecting job information. Asking standardized questions results in answers that can be of benefit to you.

Pounding the pavement can lead to finding employment. Being persistent will result in interviews and ultimate employment.

POUNDING THE PAVEMENT TOOL

After locating an industrial or business section in your community, use a criss-cross search pattern when going from company to company, making sure to record all of your visits. The POUNDING THE PAVEMENT TOOL is for this purpose. By filling in the required information at the time of visitation, you will have accurate records which will prevent visiting a company more than once. Visiting a company once is excellent . . . but after you visit ten companies they can begin to look alike. Accidently going back to the same company twice can be embarrasing.

Page 106 illustrates how your visitations would be recorded on the POUNDING THE PAVEMENT TOOL.

Additional blank copies of the POUNDING THE PAVEMENT TOOL are provided at the back of this book on page 246.

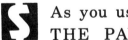

KEY CONCEPT

As you use the POUNDING THE PAVEMENT TECHNIQUE (going from company to company), be sure to record all data on the POUNDING THE PAVEMENT TOOL. This data can be used for follow-up phone calls or visits.

POUNDING THE PAVEMENT TOOL

1. Date: **9·15·81** Company/Firm Name: **STELLIT MFG**
   Address: **7261 BROUNT ST.**
   Contact Person: **BILL SMITH**   Phone: **581·6926**
   ☐ Follow-Up   ☑ Application   ☑ Resume   ☐ Interview

2. Date: **9·15·81** Company/Firm Name: **BENNINGS MFG**
   Address: **7260 BROUNT ST**
   Contact Person: **MRS CAROL VONES** Phone: **581·2113**
   ☐ Follow-Up   ☑ Application   ☑ Resume   ☐ Interview

3. Date: **9·15·81** Company/Firm Name: **RAVEN INSURANCE**
   Address: **7421 BROUNT ST**
   Contact Person: **BILL VONES**   Phone: **581-2938**
   ☐ Follow-Up   ☐ Application   ☐ Resume   ☐ Interview

4. Date: **9·15·81** Company/Firm Name: **SHELL TOIL**
   Address: **7310 BROUNT ST**
   Contact Person: **MRS SMITH**   Phone: **581-2916**
   ☑ Follow-Up **9-20** ☑ Application   ☑ Resume   ☑ Interview

5. Date: **9-15-81** Company/Firm Name: **GILMAN GRAPHICS**
   Address: **7622 BROUNT ST**
   Contact Person: **MS C. GILMAN**   Phone: **581-7731**
   ☑ Follow-Up **9-21** ☑ Application   ☑ Resume   ☑ Interview

6. Date: **9·15-81** Company/Firm Name: **MORRISON CORP**
   Address: **7851 BROUNT ST**
   Contact Person: **MS. B. MORRISON**   Phone: **581·7326**
   ☑ Follow-Up **9-26** ☑ Application   ☑ Resume   ☑ Interview

7. Date: **9-16·81** Company/Firm Name: **ERCOLI ENT**
   Address: **7962 BROUNT ST**
   Contact Person: **MS. V. ERCOLI**   Phone: **581·2913**
   ☐ Follow-Up   ☐ Application   ☑ Resume   ☐ Interview

LET YOUR FINGERS DO THE WALKING TECHNIQUE

Pounding the pavement may have specific limitations in your job search for several reasons . . . you may not have adequate transportation or the employment sites are spread out over a large geographical area. You may elect to use the telephone instead of visiting the company in person. Using the telephone to develop job leads is effective and can lead to excellent employment if you develop and use a script in your approach.

The following dramatization will illustrate the various TECHNIQUES and TOOLS used for this method (PHONE SEARCH TOOL, PHONE SCRIPT TOOL, and INTERVIEW INFORMATION TOOL). Remember, practice will give you poise and your performance will give you the job.

Examples of the PHONE SEARCH TOOL, page 122; PHONE SCRIPT TOOL, page 123; and INTERVIEW INFORMATION TOOL, page 124; have been filled in for your reference.

Additional blank copies are provided at the back of this book as follows: page 247, PHONE SEARCH TOOL; page 248, PHONE SCRIPT TOOL; and page 249, INTERVIEW INFORMATION TOOL.

LET YOUR FINGERS DO THE WALKING DRAMATIZATION:
A Telephone Conversation

CAST:

Mickey Moore: A mild-mannered individual desiring work.

Bill Estrada: Personnel Director who wants to hire the best people for his company.

Ms. Green: Personnel Office Secretary who wants to keep everyone happy.

SETTING:

Mickey is at home by her telephone with a copy of *THE JOB-SEEKERS' BIBLE*. Mr. Estrada and Ms. Green are in their respective offices.

Mickey: (to herself) "I have the Yellow Pages open to the companies that I am interested in working for. I am glad I have skills as a secretary." (type 50 words per minute, filing, receptionist, phone skills) "I know what I am about to do will work with any skills.

"I have filled in the PHONE SEARCH TOOL by listing company names and phone numbers. All the companies may not be good leads, but who knows what might develop? I also have other phone numbers to add to this list from the leads I read about in Chapter 6, EMPLOYMENT OPENINGS — PLACES TO LOOK.

"Now all I have to do is call these companies and just read from my PHONE SCRIPT TOOL."

PHONE SEARCH TOOL

COMPANY	PERSON	PHONE	NOTHING AVAILABLE	CALL BACK	SEND RESUME	APPLICATION	INTERVIEW
WOOD MFG		560·1763					
WE·CAN·DO MFG		222·7624					
CENTER CORP		477·7610					
FACTORY MFG		223·3310					
X·PERTS INC		298·6188					
REARS		297·6680					
S.D. HAROLD		463·7263					
FREEDMON MFG		562·1000					
SKY TV		474·8524					
EL CAJON MFG		442·1027					
COASTAL WATER		286·0232					
LAKESIDE SCH DIST		561·7822					
AAA SALES		423·9982					

FILL OUT TOP SECTION OF INTERVIEW INFORMATION TOOL

PHONE SCRIPT TOOL

AFTER YOU DIAL THE PHONE AND THE COMPANY HAS RESPONDED:

Hello, my name is **MICKEY MOORE** .

Who is the person in charge of hiring? **✓**

Will you spell his name for me, please? **MR BILL ESTRADA**

May I speak to **MR ESTRADA** , please. Thank you.

Mickey:	"Hello, my name is Mickey Moore. Who is the person in charge of hiring?"
Ms. Green:	"Mr. Estrada is in charge of hiring."
Mickey:	"Will you spell his name for me, please?" (as she prepares to record his name under "Person" on the PHONE SEARCH TOOL as well as on the PHONE SCRIPT TOOL)

PHONE SEARCH TOOL

COMPANY	PERSON	PHONE	NOTHING AVAILABLE	CALL BACK	SEND RESUME	APPLICATION	INTERVIEW
WOOD MFG.	MR. ESTRADA	560-1763					

Ms. Green:	"Certainly. E-S-T-R-A-D-A."
Mickey:	"Thank you. May I speak to Mr. Estrada, please?"
Ms. Green:	"Certainly. I will connect you."
Mickey:	"Thank you." (thinking to herself that if the secretary had not given out Mr. Estrada's name she would have asked if she could come in and fill out an application)

(after the connection has been made)

Mr. Estrada: "Hello. This is Mr. Estrada . . . what can I do for you?"

PHONE SCRIPT TOOL

AFTER YOU DIAL THE PHONE AND THE COMPANY HAS RESPONDED:

Hello, my name is _MICKEY MOORE_ .

Who is the person in charge of hiring? _✓_

Will you spell his name for me, please? _MR BILL ESTRADA_

May I speak to _MR. ESTRADA_ , please. Thank you.

AFTER THE CONNECTION HAS BEEN MADE:

Hello, _MR. ESTRADA_ . My name is _MICKEY MOORE_ .

(RESPONSE #1)   _TYPE. 50 WPM_
FILE, STD EQUIP

I have _5_ years experience as _A SECRETARY RECEPTIONIST/_
TELEPHONE

I am interested in a position with your company.

JOB-SEEKER RESPONSE #1:

Mickey: "Hello, Mr. Estrada. My name is Mickey Moore. I have five years of experience as a secretary and can type 50 words per minute, file, operate standard office equipment proficiently, and have receptionist telephone skills. I am interested in a position with your company."

┌─── KEY CONCEPT ───┐

Include your work background and skills when you inquire about a specific job. Limit yourself to ten seconds with this part of your script.

or

AFTER THE CONNECTION HAS BEEN MADE:

Hello, _MR ESTRADA_____. My name is _MICKEY MOORE___.

(RESPONSE #2)

    I have just completed a vocational training program and have _____

_____SECRETARIAL_____ entry level skills.

I _TYPE 50 WPM, FILE, OPERATE STD OFC EQUIP & HAVE_

_____RECEPTIONIST TELEPHONE SKILLS_____

I am interested in any entry level _SECRETARIAL_____

position you might have available.

JOB-SEEKER RESPONSE #2:

Mickey: "Hello, Mr. Estrada. My name is Mickey Moore. I have just completed a vocational training program and have entry level secretarial skills. I type 50 words per minute, file, operate most standard office equipment, and have receptionist telephone skills. I am interested in any entry level secretarial position you might have available."

KEY CONCEPT

Emphasize the completion of a training program and the skills acquired for a specific job. Limit yourself to ten seconds with this part of your script.

or

AFTER THE CONNECTION HAS BEEN MADE:

Hello, **MR ESTRADA**_____ . My name is **MICKEY MOORE**___ .

(RESPONSE #3)

I am interested in applying for any entry level **RECEPTIONIST**_____

_____position you might have available.

JOB-SEEKER RESPONSE #3:

Mickey: "Hello, Mr. Estrada. My name is
                   Mickey Moore. I am interested in
                   applying for any entry level recep-
                   tionist position you might have
                   available. I have good telephone
                   manners and work habits."

KEY CONCEPT

If you have no work experience or recent training, mention your strong points relative to a specific job. Try to limit yourself to ten seconds.

COMPANY RESPONSE #1:

Mr. Estrada: "Yes, we have an opening. Would you come in for an interview?" (Mr. Estrada appreciates Mickey's business-like approach and is impressed with her brief conversation)

PHONE SCRIPT TOOL

IF POSITIVE RESPONSE: Fill in top section of INTERVIEW INFORMATION TOOL.

INTERVIEW INFORMATION TOOL

WHAT YOU MUST KNOW BEFORE THE INTERVIEW:

Day: _____ Date: _____ Time: _____

Company Name: **WOOD MANUFACTURING COMPANY**

Address: _____

Interviewer's Name: **MR ESTRADA** Title: _____

Room Number: _____ Phone Number: _____ Extension: _____

Transportation: _____ Parking: _____

Major Facts About the Company: _____

_____

Job You Want at This Company: _____

Mickey: (as she places the INTERVIEW INFORMATION TOOL in front of her to record the necessary information) "Yes, certainly. Can you give me the day and time?"

Mickey is on her way to a positive and excellent interview situation!

Suppose, however, that Mr. Estrada responded in the following manner:

COMPANY RESPONSE #2:

PHONE SCRIPT TOOL

IF NEGATIVE RESPONSE:

May I come in and fill out an application or send you my resume? $(10\frac{00}{AM})$

☑ YES RESPONSE: When would be a good time to come in? $8:\frac{30}{AM} - 3\frac{30}{PM}$

Mr. Estrada:	"I have no openings at this time."
Mickey:	"May I come in and fill out an application or send you my resume?"
Mr. Estrada:	"Yes, please do." (impressed with her thoroughness)
Mickey:	"When would be a good time to come in?" (The appropriate box is checked on the PHONE SEARCH TOOL.)

PHONE SEARCH TOOL

COMPANY	PERSON	PHONE	NOTHING AVAILABLE	CALL BACK	SEND RESUME	APPLICATION	INTERVIEW
WOOD MFG.	MR ESTRADA	560-1763				✓ 8:30-3:30	

Mr. Estrada:	"Any time between 8:30 a.m. and 3:30 p.m. is appropriate."
Mickey:	"Thank you for your time and effort, Mr. Estrada. I will come in tomorrow at 10:00 a.m. and apply. Have a nice day."

Suppose Mr. Estrada said his company was not accepting applications at this time. The following illustrates this situation:

COMPANY RESPONSE #3:

PHONE SCRIPT TOOL

IF NEGATIVE RESPONSE:

May I come in and fill out an application or send you my resume?

☐ YES RESPONSE: When would be a good time to come in?_____

☑ NO RESPONSE: May I call you again . . . say in a couple weeks? __YES__

Mr. Estrada: "We are not accepting applications at this time."

Mickey: "May I call you again . . . say in a couple weeks?"

Mr. Estrada: "Yes . . . in a couple of weeks."

(Mickey also fills in the appropriate box on the PHONE SEARCH TOOL.)

PHONE SEARCH TOOL

COMPANY	PERSON	PHONE	NOTHING AVAILABLE	CALL BACK	SEND RESUME	APPLICATION	INTERVIEW
WOOD MFG	MR. ESTRADA	560·1763		✓ 3·12			
WE·CAN· DO MFG		222·7644					
CENTER CORP		477·7710					
FACTORY MFG		223-3310					
X·PERTS INC		298·6188					

PHONE SCRIPT TOOL

☑ NO RESPONSE: May I call you again . . . say in a couple weeks? _YES_

Do you know of any company with openings at this time that could benefit from my skills? _MARSHALL CO - JOE CAMAH 333·4455_

Mickey:	(realizing Mr. Estrada now knows her and was impressed by her phone techniques . . .) "Mr. Estrada, do you know of any company with openings at this time that could benefit from my skills?"
Mr. Estrada:	"Why, yes . . . Marshall Company just down the steet from us is looking for a receptionist. Joe Camah is in charge there at 333-4455. Why don't you give him a call?"

(Mickey also lists the Marshall Company, Joe Camah, and his phone number on the PHONE SEARCH TOOL and the phone script approach begins again.)

PHONE SEARCH TOOL

COMPANY	PERSON	PHONE	NOTHING AVAILABLE	CALL BACK	SEND RESUME	APPLICATION	INTERVIEW
COASTAL WATER		286·0232					
LAKESIDE SCH DIST		561-7822					
AAA SALES		423·9982					
MARSHALL CO	JOE CAMAH	333-4455					

or

PHONE SCRIPT TOOL

Do you know of any company with openings at this time that could benefit from my skills? ___NO___

Thank you very much for your time and consideration. I hope to talk to you again.

Mr. Estrada: "I do not know of anyone who is hiring at this time."

Mickey: "Thank you very much for your time and consideration, Mr. Estrada. I hope to talk to you again."

KEY CONCEPT

1. Develop a short script according to your skills and/or desires. Write it out on the PHONE SCRIPT TOOL and stick to it.

2. Try to keep the major part of your delivery to ten seconds in length.

3. Practice your script with a friend or relative over the phone until you are good at it.

4. Use the PHONE SEARCH TOOL to write down 20 prospective company names and phone numbers. List them in reverse order so the place you would *least* like to work is first. As you develop your phone skills, this reverse order allows you to practice for the calls that really count.

5. Pick up the phone receiver and do not put it down until you have dialed and talked to all 20 prospective employers. If you put it down, it is difficult to pick up again.

6. If you do make a mistake and become flustered, just hang up. After you regain your composure, call back again and say, "We must have been disconnected."

7. Have the INTERVIEW INFORMATION TOOL ready in case you get a "bite." Record all the information in the top section ("WHAT YOU MUST KNOW BEFORE THE INTERVIEW"). Chapter 8 elaborates on this TOOL.

SUMMARY

Purposeful and directive effort is necessary to succeed in finding employment openings. Develop a network system by enlisting the aid of friends, relatives and neighbors to help you find employment openings. Visit company personnel or employment offices. Use the PHONE SEARCH TOOL along with the PHONE SCRIPT TOOL for a unique telephone approach to job-seeking. Use the *Business Directory* of your local Chamber of Commerce. Ask members and leaders at church about any job leads. Check with the placement offices of the Employment Development Department, schools, and the federal, state, county, or city government. Check the newspaper, labor unions, and/or private employment agencies. Consider the temporary or casual labor market as an effective way to earn quick money and possible full-time employment.

If looking for out-of-town employment, collect information about the area, send letters of application including a resume to companies that appeal to you, and avoid moving your belongings until you have "trial worked" a job or at least been given written assurance of a position.

When using the telephone to find employment openings, practice a well-developed script and be brief. You should receive two positive responses for every ten telephone inquiries. For this purpose, use the PHONE SEARCH TOOL (example on page 122), the PHONE SCRIPT TOOL (example on page 123), and the INTER-VIEW INFORMATION TOOL: WHAT YOU MUST KNOW BEFORE THE INTERVIEW (example on page 124). The INTERVIEW INFORMATION TOOL would be filled in if you were asked to come in to "interview." This TOOL is fully explained in Chapter 8.

Additional blank copies of each of these TOOLS are provided at the back of this book on pages 247, 248, and 249.

PHONE SEARCH TOOL

COMPANY	PERSON	PHONE	NOTHING AVAILABLE	CALL BACK	SEND RESUME	APPLICATION	INTERVIEW
WOOD MFG CO	MR BILL ESTRADA	560-1763				✓ HOURS 8:30-3:30	
WE-CAN-DO MFG CO	MR JOHN JONES	222-7644					✗
CENTER CORP	MS PAUL	477-7710	✓ OUT OF BUSINESS				
FACTORY MFG	MR BOWES	223-3310	✓	✓ 2 WEEKS 3-3-20			
X-PERTS INC	MS LITTLE	298-6188					
REARS	MR MONTCLAIR	297-6680	✓			✓ HOURS 9:00-5:00	✗
S.D HAROLD	SALLY	463-7263					
FREEDMON MFG	MRS BLACK	562-1000	✓ REFERRED TO MARSHALL				
SKY TV	MR SKY	474-1027	✓ NO OFFICE STAFF				
EL CAJON CO	MRS KING	442-8524		✓ TOMORROW 3-4			
COASTAL WATER	MR BILL MEANS	286-0232					
LAKESIDE SCHOOL DIST	MS KATE CLOCK	561-7822				✓ HOURS 8:15-5:00	
AAA SALES	MR HATFIELD	423-9982		✓ 1 WEEK 3-10			
MARSHALL	MR JOE CAMAH	333-4455					✗

FILL OUT TOP SECTION
OF **INTERVIEW INFORMATION TOOL**

PHONE SCRIPT TOOL

AFTER YOU DIAL THE PHONE AND THE COMPANY HAS RESPONDED:

Hello, my name is __MICKEY MOORE__.

Who is the person in charge of hiring? __✓__

Will you spell his name for me, please? __MR BILL ESTRADA__

May I speak to __MR ESTRADA__, please. Thank you.

AFTER THE CONNECTION HAS BEEN MADE:

Hello, __MR ESTRADA__. My name is __MICKEY MOORE__.

(RESPONSE #1)

I have __5__ years experience as __A SECRETARY__.

I am interested in a position with your company.

or

(RESPONSE #2)

I have just completed a vocational training program and have _____

__SECRETARIAL__ entry level skills.

I __TYPE 50 WPM, FILE, STD OFC EQUIP, PHONE,__.

I am interested in any entry level _____

position you might have available.

or

(RESPONSE #3)

I am interested in applying for any entry level __RECEPTIONIST__

_____ position you might have available.

IF POSITIVE RESPONSE:

Fill in top section of INTERVIEW INFORMATION TOOL.

IF NEGATIVE RESPONSE:

May I come in and fill out an application or send you my resume?

☑ YES RESPONSE: When would be a good time to come in? __8 30 AM · 3 30 PM (10 00 AM)__

☑ NO RESPONSE: May I call you again . . . say in a couple weeks? __YES__

Do you know of any company with openings at this time that could benefit from my skills? __MARSHALL CO - JOE CAMAH · 333-4455__

Thank you very much for your time and consideration. I hope to talk to you again.

INTERVIEW INFORMATION TOOL

WHAT YOU MUST KNOW **BEFORE** THE INTERVIEW:

Day: **FRIDAY**   Date: **MARCH 5**   Time: **9 $\frac{00}{AM}$**

Company Name: **MARSHALL**

Address: **814 PEACH · EL CAJON**

Interviewer's Name: **JOE CAMAH**   Title: **PRESIDENT**

Room Number: **4**   Phone Number: _____ Extension: _____

Transportation: **BUS #5**   Parking: _____

Major Facts About the Company: **PUBLISHING COMPANY**

JUST BEGINNING NEW BRANCH OFFICE

Job You Want at This Company: **SECRETARY**

WHAT YOU MUST ASK **DURING** THE INTERVIEW:

Jobs Discussed During the Interview: _____

Job Duties: _____

Rate of Pay: _____

Raises/Pay/Increases: _____

Fringe Benefits: _____

Opportunities for Advancement: _____

On-The-Job Training: _____

Work Schedule: _____

Breaks: _____ nch: _____

When Will I Know? _____

May I Call You? _____ When? _____

TO BE DISCUSSED IN CHAPTER 8

THANK YOU.

Notes: _____

CHAPTER 7

First Impression

WOMEN

Attire
Makeup
Hair
Scent

MEN

Attire
Hair
Hands
Scent

First Impression

Your first impression is important because you will never have a second chance to make that FIRST impression.

In less than 1/10th of one second we can totally observe a person and have an opinion about them. This is subliminal (occurs in our subconscious) but, nevertheless, does occur. Subliminal advertising was used by movie theatres to induce patrons to buy more snacks. It worked! A single frame of an individual eating would be flashed on the screen and through subliminal perception increased snack sales by 200%.

When you appear in an employment office, you make your FIRST impression. It takes about 1/10th of a second to look at you, your dress . . . your complete person. If that first impression is GOOD, the first three minutes of the interview can be spent illustrating your potential to an already impressed interviewer. However, if that first impression is poor, you will spend your next three minutes trying to impress the interviewer.

What is so important about the first three minutes? That is how long it takes most prospective employers to decide to hire you . . . or not to hire you. Even though the interview may take longer, most employers agree that the first three minutes are the most important during the interview process.

The following constitutes a GOOD FIRST IMPRESSION:

WOMEN

Your appearance is your first impression. Your appearance consists of attire (including colors), make-up, hair, and scent.

ATTIRE

Appropriate dress is basic to gaining employment. Because most personnel offices are relatively conservative, a conservative style of dress is your best bet. The SAFEST BET is a dress with sleeves, low-heeled closed-toed shoes, nylons, and a sweater or jacket (if necessary). A suit (jacket, blouse, and skirt) is even better. Pant suits or slacks are not always acceptable. A dress or a suit is! Whether you are applying for a welding job or an office job, applying in a dress (or a suit) is always a safe bet. Take along a pair of coveralls if you are going for a try-out in a shop. You can change at the place of employment AFTER you are invited to give a work sample. Good grooming is an asset regardless of what kind of job you are applying for.

Your attire should be conservative, complimentary, and stylish . . . but not to the degree that your appearance threatens all the other female help or over-stimulates all of the male help. Employers are primarily interested in productivity and anything or anybody that threatens that productivity will be excluded.

If you cannot afford a new outfit, you can still have one if you do a little research. Select the best women's apparel store in town and go in there as if you were going to buy them out. Allow one of their experts to dress you in clothes that compliment you regardless of price. After you have identified a dress or a suit that compliments you, tell the salesperson that you have to do some more shopping. Then, go to a thrift store, or any other second hand store, and select a similar dress or suit at 1/10th the cost. Perform the necessary minor alterations, if needed, and you have your "Job-Seeking Outfit." (After you are gainfully employed, you can go back to that women's apparel store and afford to buy clothes there.)

Wear your "Job-Seeking Outfit" only when job-seeking because you know when you look your best . . . you will do your best. Do not wear these special clothes to the Saturday Disco. Come bright and early Monday morning you may get a call for an interview . . . and there you have a "wine and dine" stain right down your front! There goes your chance for a good interview due to sheer panic. If you can afford two outfits . . . all the better . . . for you will have one in reserve. One suit with three blouses will give you variety at a moderate price.

Hose with subtle tones will compliment your conservative dress. Carry an extra pair of hose in your purse in case you get a "run" while you are away from home.

Your clothes should be clean, well-pressed, and have all the buttons firmly attached.

Earth tones, browns, blues, and grays are success colors. Studies and surveys indicate that the most successful people wear these colors. Illustrate your planned success by wearing these colors NOW.

MAKE-UP

Cosmetics should be used sparingly and the colors should match. That is . . . nail polish, lipstick, and rouge must all be of the same tone. Conservative make-up or the natural look is excellent. Remember that most office settings are brighter than your bathroom . . . so make-up that is bright at home will be gaudy in the interview. Heavy eyeliner and heavy eye shadow should be avoided.

HAIR

Exotic hairdos and wigs (unless you have scalp damage) are obvious in a bright office. A well-groomed and styled haircut is appropriate and indicates cleanliness and efficiency. A hair style that calls attention to the wearer is always safe while elaborate hair styles that call attention to the hair will limit your chances for employment. If you cannot afford a regular salon appointment, find a beauty college. By paying a little more, you can request an advanced student. Allow them the final decision for your hair design for they are trained for that.

SCENT

Scent should be subtle or non-existent. Interviewing offices are usually small and heavy perfumes will be too strong for the interview. If the scent can be smelled, it is too strong. Be sure to use deodorant because nervousness increases perspiration. Deodorant should be used in addition to . . . not instead of . . . bathing.

KEY CONCEPT

Your appearance is your FIRST IMPRESSION . . . make it a good one because it will be worth thousands of dollars to you in terms of income through job procurement.

MEN

Your appearance is your FIRST IMPRESSION. Your appearance consists of attire (including color choice), hair, hands, and scent.

ATTIRE

Appropriate attire is basic to gaining employment. A sport coat and a tie are never out of place when applying for a job. The outfit should be clean, pressed, and have matching tones.

A pair of coveralls or a change of clothes should be carried with you in case you "try-out" in a shop.

Polished shoes or boots will illustrate your attention to detail . . . a quality admired by employers.

A three-piece suit is excellent for professional interviews or management level applications. In most technical areas a person in a three-piece suit appears overdressed where the sport coat/blazer and tie are always acceptable.

If you cannot tolerate a tie and are applying for a technical job, a clean, neat, open shirt is a reasonable alternate.

Men can purchase excellent clothes (if you are a careful shopper) at a second hand clothing store for 1/10th the regular purchase price.

Keep your "Job-Hunting Clothes" specifically for that . . . job-hunting. Avoid wearing them to the beer bust because in a small interview office you will smell like old smoke and stale beer!

Studies and surveys indicate that the most successful people wear earth tones . . . browns, blues and grays . . . the success colors. Illustrate your planned success by wearing these colors NOW.

HAIR

Haircuts and permanents can be expensive. Find a beauty college if you cannot afford a regular salon treatment. Request an advanced student. Allow them the final decision for your hair design for they are trained for it.

A conservative (short) hair length will give you your best shot at a job as well as a well-trimmed beard, if you have one. After you have worked at a company and they are confident in your skills, you can let your hair and/or beard grow longer.

HANDS and SCENT

Hands and nails should be as clean and well-groomed as possible. Aftershave lotion or cologne should not be strong or overwhelming. Be sure to use deodorant, because nervousness increases perspiration. Deodorant should be used in addition to . . . not instead of . . . bathing.

KEY CONCEPT

Your appearance is your FIRST IMPRESSION . . . so make it a good one because it will be worth thousands of dollars to you in terms of income through job procurement.

SUMMARY

In 1/10th of a second an interviewer gets that first impression of you. In three minutes the interviewer will decide whether or not he or she wants to hire you. Your total appearance is your FIRST IMPRESSION.

CHAPTER 8

The Interview

WHAT IT IS

INTERVIEW INFORMATION TOOL

Before The Interview

WHAT TO DO

INTERVIEW INFORMATION TOOL

During The Interview

INTERVIEW DRAMATIZATION

WHAT TO BRING

POST INTERVIEW TECHNIQUES

Thank-You Notes
Telephone Follow-up

The Interview

WHAT IT IS

An interview is a discussion between a potential employee and a potential employer's representative regarding employment. Both informal and formal discussion TECHNIQUES are utilized so that both participants can collect enough data to make a rational decision regarding the employment position.

The major emphasis is to collect data. Both of the participants must ask enough relevant questions so that each can determine the appropriateness of the job relative to their viewpoint. Based on that data, the potential employer may or may not want to hire the potential employee. However, based on that same data, the potential employee may or may not want to work for the employer.

Interviewing is no different than acting on a stage. The interviewer asks certain questions and you will "perform" with an answer. If you "perform" appropriately, you will probably have the job . . . just as a show person receives applause. It is no more complex than that!

People go to see actors/actresses because they like them and you will be hired because prospective employers like you! Of course, you must have the prerequisite skills to perform the job but basically you are hired because you are liked. Prospective employers will like and hire you because of your appearance, your interest in them (or what they stand for), and the way you present yourself.

INTERVIEW INFORMATION TOOL
BEFORE THE INTERVIEW

The INTERVIEW INFORMATION TOOL is a most important TOOL for job-seeking success. It will assist you before and during the interview to collect valuable job information while you favorably impress a potential employer.

The upper section of the INTERVIEW INFORMATION TOOL will assist you in gaining the necessary information needed BEFORE an interview. An example INTERVIEW INFORMATION TOOL has been filled in for your reference on page 149. Additional blank copies of this TOOL are provided at the end of this book on page 249.

Refer to a blank INTERVIEW INFORMATION TOOL as you go through the following information:

INTERVIEW INFORMATION TOOL

WHAT YOU MUST KNOW **BEFORE** THE INTERVIEW:

Day: **WEDNESDAY**   Date: **OCT 21**   Time: **9:00 AM**

DAY/DATE/TIME:

Write down the exact interview day of the week, date, and time while making interview arrangements. Repeat the information back to whomever is giving you the appointment.

Make sure there is no miscommunication by him or her . . . or by you. It is embarrassing to show up for the interview two days early or three hours late!

INTERVIEW INFORMATION TOOL

WHAT YOU MUST KNOW **BEFORE** THE INTERVIEW:

Day: _WEDNESDAY_   Date: _OCT 21_   Time: _9:00 AM_

Company Name: _WE · CAN · DO MFG_

Address: _314 ROSEWOOD S.D._

COMPANY NAME and ADDRESS:

Make sure the COMPANY NAME is correctly spelled. It is not uncommon for one personnel office to do the hiring for two or more subsidiary plants or organizations.

Write down the ADDRESS of where the interview will take place. A company may have many locations, but probably only one employment office.

INTERVIEW INFORMATION TOOL

WHAT YOU MUST KNOW **BEFORE** THE INTERVIEW:

Day: _WEDNESDAY_   Date: _OCT 21_   Time: _9:00 AM_

Company Name: _WE·CAN· DO MFG_

Address: _314 ROSEWOOD   S.D_

Interviewer's Name: _MR JONES_   Title: _PERSONNEL DIRECTOR_

Room Number: _MAIN PERS OFC_   Phone Number: _222·7644_   Extension: _98_

INTERVIEWER'S NAME/TITLE/ROOM NUMBER/ PHONE/EXTENSION:

Obtain the correct spelling and pronounciation of the INTERVIEWER'S NAME and TITLE. Practice saying the name so you can call the interviewer by name when meeting him or her. Always record Mr. (pronounced "Mister"), Mrs. (pronounced "Missus"), Ms. (pronounced "Mizz"), or Dr. (pronounced "Doctor"). If you forget how to pronounce the last name, you can call the secretary for a correct pronunciation. Greeting a person by name is impressive and will mean positive "job points" for you!

Record the ROOM NUMBER. Office buildings have elevators and directories that can be confusing. The room number will get you to the right floor and room without frustration.

Check to make sure you have the correct PHONE NUMBER and EXTENSION of the interviewer . . . it may be different from the company phone number recorded on the previously discussed PHONE SEARCH TOOL (Chapter 6).

INTERVIEW INFORMATION TOOL

WHAT YOU MUST KNOW **BEFORE** THE INTERVIEW:

Day: _WEDNESDAY_ Date: _OCT 21_ Time: _9:00 AM_

Company Name: _WE·CAN·DO MFG_

Address: _341 ROSEWOOD S.D._

Interviewer's Name: _MR JONES_ Title: _PERSONNEL DIRECTOR_

Room Number: _MAIN PERS SEC_ Phone Number: _222-7644_ Extension: _98_

Transportation: _CAR_ Parking: _VISITORS LOT # 1_

TRANSPORTATION/PARKING:

Parking arrangements must be made in advance at some companies. In large cities you may have to pay for your parking . . . so always have money available.

If you take the bus or a train, double check the schedule to make sure you have read it correctly. Have extra tokens and change. Be sure to ask for a transfer if needed.

If you go by taxi, allow enough lead time because taxis do not have schedules to keep like other forms of transportation.

The object of TRANSPORTATION and PARKING is to ensure your safe, timely and unruffled arrival at the correct interview site.

INTERVIEW INFORMATION TOOL

WHAT YOU MUST KNOW **BEFORE** THE INTERVIEW:

Day: WEDNESDAY   Date: OCT 21   Time: 9:00 AM

Company Name: WE· CAN· DO MFG

Address: 311 ROSEWOOD S.D.

Interviewer's Name: MR JONES   Title: PERSONNEL DIRECTOR

Room Number: MAIN PERS OFC   Phone Number: 222-7644 Extension: 98

Transportation: CAR   Parking: VISITORS LOT #1

Major Facts About the Company: ALUMINUN CAN MANUFACTURERS DOING BUSINESS FOR 20 YEARS · 2000 EMPLOYEES

MAJOR FACTS ABOUT THE COMPANY:

Briefly record important FACTS about the com-pany. Collect this information by talking with friends, using the Yellow Pages, procuring a policy booklet from the company, asking the secretary, or using the *Business Directory* at the Chamber of Commerce (refer to Chapter 6 under PLACES TO LOOK Section).

FACTS can include: products, services, associated companies, subsidiaries, number of employees, physical plant size, yearly gross in dollars, reputation, and friends who are employees.

You will favorably impress the interviewer by know-ing something about the company. Record the facts so you can keep them straight in the interview. Facts have a way of blending together and could cause you embar-rassment if you just trust them to memory. You may want to take a few minutes to review these facts just before arriving for your interview.

INTERVIEW INFORMATION TOOL

WHAT YOU MUST KNOW **BEFORE** THE INTERVIEW:

Day: _WEDNESDAY_ Date: _OCT 21_ Time: _9:00 AM_

Company Name: _WE·CAN·DO MFG_

Address: _341 ROSEWOOD S.D._

Interviewer's Name: _MR JONES_ Title: _PERSONNEL DIRECTOR_

Room Number: _MAIN OFC_ Phone Number: _222-7644_ Extension: _98_

Transportation: _CAR_ Parking: _VISITORS LOT #1_

Major Facts About the Company: _ALUMINUM CAN MANUFACTURERS_ _DOING BUSINESS FOR 20 YEARS. 2000 EMPLOYEES_

Job You Want at This Company: _CLERK TYPIST_

JOB YOU WANT AT THIS COMPANY:

People who ask for "anything that is open" usually get nothing!

Busy interviewers do not have time to counsel you to see where you would fit in their company. Interviewers are interested in people who know what they want so that employment decisions can be made. It may be true that you will take anything, but always apply for s-o-m-e-t-h-i-n-g! Specify janitor, custodian, stock clerk, machinist trainee, mechanical assembler, receptionist, marketing secretary, or any other job that you think is available. (Many hours are wasted by job-seekers who apply for jobs that are not related to the industry where they are making application.) Remember, you can upgrade or downgrade your job request during the interview.

KEY CONCEPT

The INTERVIEW INFORMA-TION TOOL is an important TOOL for job-seeking success. The top section (WHAT YOU MUST KNOW **BEFORE** THE INTERVIEW) is for recording the date, time, and place an interview is to take place along with the interviewer's name, title, room number, and telephone number. Transportation and parking information may also be noted. Record some major facts about the company and have a specific job in mind.

INTERVIEW INFORMATION TOOL

WHAT YOU MUST KNOW **BEFORE** THE INTERVIEW:

Day: _WEDNESDAY_ Date: _OCT 21_ Time: _9:88 AM_

Company Name: _WE·CAN·DO MFG_

Address: _3411 ROSEWOOD   S.D._

Interviewer's Name: _MR JONES_ Title: _PERSONNEL DIRECTOR_

Room Number: _MAIN PERS OFC_ Phone Number: _222-7614_ Extension: _C18_

Transportation: _CAR_ Parking: _VISITORS LOT # 1_

Major Facts About the Company: _ALUMINUM CAN MANUFACTURERS_
DOING BUSINESS FOR 20 YEARS. 2000 EMPLOYEES

Job You Want at This Company: _CLERK TYPIST_

WHAT YOU MUST KNOW **DURING** THE INTERVIEW:

Jobs Discussed During the Interview: _____

Job Duties: _____

Rate of Pay: _____

Raises/Pay/Increases: _____

Fringe Benefits: _____

Opportunities for Advancement: _____

On-The-Job Training: _____

Work Schedule: _____

Breaks: _____ nch: _____

When Will I Know? _____

May I Call You? _____ When? _____

THANK YOU.

Notes: _____
_____
_____
_____
_____
_____
_____
_____

TO BE DISCUSSED LATER

WHAT TO DO

1. ARRIVE AT LEAST 15 MINUTES EARLY

   This will give you time to fill out an application by copying from your APPLICATION INFORMA-TION TOOL (Chapter 5). Being early also illustrates your promptness and helps you to avoid that rushed feeling.

2. RELAX AND WAIT YOUR TURN

   Relaxing is easier said than done. If you use the following TECHNIQUES, you will make yourself feel much better:

   a. Rub your throat with your hand.

      The trauma of the interview literally puts you into shock. The blood vessels in your throat constrict and you are afraid you will make a "Disney character sound" when you speak. Rubbing your throat causes the blood vessels to relax, thereby ensuring that your vocal tones will be normal.

   b. Take a deep breath.

      Most of you tend to breathe less deeply when you are anxious or nervous. This robs the body of that all-important oxygen supply. Lack of oxygen adds to your feeling of insecurity. The resolution is easy . . . concentrate on deep, even breathing.

c. Rub your hands together.

Release tension by firmly rubbing your hands together. Your body has been tensed up with adrenalin (the natural hormone that fortifies your body for a traumatic event). The glands usually give you more adrenalin than you need. (If you were running from a hungry lion, the adrenalin supplied would be adequate . . . hopefully . . . but you are just sitting in an office.) This excess should be worked off, thus releasing some pressure. Rubbing your hands together is a remarkable way to relieve these pressures.

d. Tighten and loosen your upper leg muscles.

Sitting near the edge of a chair and tightening and loosening your upper leg muscles (as if you were getting ready to stand up), is another excellent way to relax. The upper leg muscles constitute the largest muscle group in the body and flexing them releases the adrenalin . . . thereby relieving the anxiety.

All the forementioned stress relievers and relaxation TECHNIQUES can be done in the office without attracting attention. Before leaving home, walk briskly, jog, or exercise. This will make you feel better.

3. GIVE THE SECRETARY YOUR HIGHEST REGARD

When you enter the office be friendly and courteous. The secretary will probably introduce you to the interviewer. Her body language (as interpreted by her boss — the interviewer) will give the interviewer a clue as to how she sees you. The secretary has the power to compliment or degrade you with just a subtle glance, raised eyebrow, or facial expression. She, in some cases, can make or break you.

4. INTRODUCTION TO INTERVIEWER
   a. Eye Contact

   Look into the interviewer's eyes. Eye contact denotes trust and a desire to communicate . . . and that is what you both want. Never wear sunglasses.
   b. Handshakes

   Memorize the following rules:
   1) Male applicant to male interviewer

   If you are a male applicant, you should extend your hand at the beginning and at the end of the interview for a firm handshake. Wait until you are asked to be seated and use other appropriate courtesies.

2) Male applicant to female interviewer

If you are a male applicant, allow the female interviewer to initiate courtesies. IF she extends her hand, a handshake is appropriate. You may hold the door and always wait until you are asked to be seated.

3) Female applicant to male interviewer

If you are a female applicant, extend your hand to the male interviewer both before and after the interview (if you desire). Receive the courtesies that are extended. You may be seated without being asked.

4) Female applicant to female interviewer

If you are a female applicant, ALWAYS allow the female interviewer to control all aspects of courtesy. That is, let her extend her hand for the handshake and allow her to offer you a seat. If she indicates, you can pass through the door first. If not, let her pass through first. The concluding handshake should also be determined by the female interviewer.

c. If you have a physical handicap, be up front about it in order to put your interviewer at ease.

5. POSTURE

Sit straight in the chair or toward the front edge of the seat. Put your hands in your lap and clasp them together to avoid unconscious drumming of the fingers or sporadic hand movements. (Using hand gestures in conversation is acceptable.) Keep both feet on the floor to avoid that lounging look. Ladies, if crossing your legs makes you more comfortable, do so in a manner that is not revealing.

6. ORAL ACTIVITIES

Speak loudly enough to be heard and be specific with the pronunciation of your words. Be sure to smile from time to time. Be conscious of your facial expression (appropriate responses can be practiced in front of a mirror before leaving home for the interview).

A breath mint is refreshing while waiting in the outer office and can be disposed of quickly when called for the actual interview. Never chew gum, candy or mints during the interview. Surveys of employers indicate that if you smoke during the interview, you will not be hired.

7. BEGINNING INFORMATION

After you enter the interviewer's office some light conversation will usually take place:

"What is the weather like out there?"

"Did you have any problems finding our company?"

This is the interviewer's attempt to make you comfortable. The following is an acceptable response to the interviewer's courtesy question:

"It is a beautiful day and I am glad to be here, but to be honest with you, I am really nervous."

Interviewers will respond in a kind and supportive fashion that will reassure you, thus making you more comfortable and less nervous. Just stating the fact you are nervous often eliminates the problem. If no supportive comment is made, you will get a clue as to the type of company it is.

After a couple of minutes, the interviewer will shift to the business at hand . . . interviewing.

8. WHEN YOU ARE ASKED QUESTIONS

Answer all questions honestly and openly. You can stop for a couple of seconds to organize your thoughts. You do not have to be instantaneous with your responses. NEVER talk about yourself for more than one minute. You can practice timing yourself (explained in Chapter 3 on page 34) by responding to the given questions while observing your watch. If you talk longer than one minute you will probably ramble, repeat yourself, and/or bring up weak points in your background that are not complimentary to you.

Always be honest . . . then you can concentrate on answering the question at hand and not try to remember what you have already said.

a. Answering Trick Questions

The answers to trick questions are not what the interviewer desires . . . your reaction is what he or she is after. (Refer to Chapter 3, page 32, entitled TRICK QUESTIONS — General.)

b. Answering Technical Questions

Technical questions require knowledgeable answers and usually only one correct answer exists. You should answer the question if you are positive of the correct answer, but do not guess. An appropriate response would be:

"I don't have that information at hand, but I know where I can find out quickly."

(Refer to Chapter 3, page 42, entitled, TRICK QUESTIONS — Technical.)

c. Questions Regarding Past Employment

Always be complimentary about your past employers. You have left them (or are in the process of leaving them) because of your quest for one of the following reasons:

"a greater challenge in a job"

or

"improved salary or fringe benefits"

or

"career advantages with another company."

Even if you hate a past employer, your interview is not a good time to share your hatred.

Always be positive. (Refer to Chapter 3, page 43, entitled TRICK QUESTIONS — Past Employment.)

9. WHEN QUESTIONS ARE ASKED

During the interview two things should occur:

(1) The company representative collects data regarding you based on information from an application, a resume, and/or the interview.

(2) You collect data about the company based on information regarding job duties, pay, raises, benefits, work schedule, advancement, etc.

The interviewer will *carefully record* information about you so that he or she can make a logical decision about you.

YOU, too, should *carefully record* information about the company so that you can also make logical decisions regarding the company.

Interviewers are complimented when you ask them, "Is it okay if I take some notes?" This makes them feel you are really interested in what they have to say.

INTERVIEW INFORMATION TOOL
DURING THE INTERVIEW

Use the bottom half of the following INTERVIEW INFORMATION TOOL as a basis for all your questions. Use the provided space to write down the obtained information just as it occurs during the interview. This ensures that you know everything regarding the job so a rational decision can be made. All information on the INTERVIEW INFORMATION TOOL is necessary for intelligent job selection.

An example INTERVIEW INFORMATION TOOL has been filled in for your reference on page 175.

Additional copies of this TOOL are provided at the end of this book on page 249.

INTERVIEW INFORMATION TOOL

WHAT YOU MUST KNOW **DURING** THE INTERVIEW·

Jobs Discussed During the Interview: <u>CLERK·TYPIST</u>
LEVEL II (SALES DEPT)

JOBS DISCUSSED DURING THE INTERVIEW:

The job you discuss during the interview may be:

The job you applied for;

or

An upgraded or downgraded version of the job applied for;

or

A totally different job from the one applied for.

Write down the technical name of the job discussed in the interview so that you can refer to it intelligently when, and if, another contact is made.

INTERVIEW INFORMATION TOOL

WHAT YOU MUST KNOW **DURING** THE INTERVIEW:

Jobs Discussed During the Interview: _CLERK TYPIST LEVEL II (SALES DEPT)_

Job Duties: TYPING, PHONES, FILING, RESEARCH, REPORTS

JOB DUTIES:

Be sure you know exactly what the job entails — exactly what will be expected of you. You may not have all of the skills required to perform the job duties. The interview is the best time to discover that . . . not the first day of work! There may be duties that your religious or ethical background will not allow you to perform . . . so now is the time to find out.

A secretary/receptionist is a standard job designation in most companies. Job duties will vary with the needs. A small company will probably expect a secretary/receptionist to do it all . . . front desk, typing, billing, phones, bank deposits, coffee runs, bookkeeping, etc. A large company may require only front office activities or exclusively "pool" typing.

Remember, you will be performing for eight hours a day so make sure you know exactly what you're getting into!

INTERVIEW INFORMATION TOOL

WHAT YOU MUST KNOW **DURING** THE INTERVIEW:

Jobs Discussed During the Interview: _CLERK· TYPIST LEVEL II (SALES DEPT)_

Job Duties: _TYPING, PHONES, FILING, RESEARCH, REPORTS_

Rate of Pay: _$5.50 PER HOUR_

RATE OF PAY:

Many people are nervous asking about the pay even if it could be the most important aspect of the job.

Request information about the hourly rate or salary. In some cases the pay range is adequate. Be certain to narrow down the pay range to a specific amount before you make a final commitment.

Recording the RATE OF PAY has other advantages. Suppose you hire into a company and agree on an hourly rate of $5.50. After you receive your first check you discover that it breaks down to only $5.00 an hour. If you have recorded the hourly rate during the interview, you can approach your supervisor or the personnel officer to resolve the issue. It could be an honest mistake or the company could be doing that to all their employees to save paying the extra $0.50 per hour.

INTERVIEW INFORMATION TOOL

Jobs Discussed During the Interview: <u>CLERK TYPIST LEVEL II (SALES DEPT)</u>

Job Duties: <u>TYPING, PHONES, FILING, RESEARCH REPORTS</u>

Rate of Pay: <u>$5.50 PER HOUR</u>

Raises/Pay/Increases: <u>90 DAY PROBATION</u>
<u>(50¢ RAISE EVERY 6 MONTHS)</u>

RAISES/PAY INCREASES:

This factor is very important to know so you can plan your financial future. All companies vary in their pay raise structure. While some companies have a 30-day probationary period with a raise upon being made a permanent employee, a firm next door may have a 90-day probationary period. Some organizations have regular standardized pay raises, others have a "merit" system, while others have no plan for raises at all!

Knowing the opportunity for raises at a company will make your decision regarding employment more data-based. For example, you could hire into Company A at $5.00 per hour with no raise plan or Company B at $4.50 per hour with a structured raise plan. You must determine the gross amount (actual wage earnings over a one-year period including taxes) before you can make a rational decision.

The following is an example of what might occur if you were offered these two jobs:

COMPANY A (No definite raise plan)

Hourly Wage	×	Hours per Week	×	Weeks per Year	=	Gross Earnings
$5.00	×	40	×	52	=	$10,400.00
						(Yearly amount before taxes)

COMPANY B (With the following structure package:

> $4.75 per hour the first 4 weeks
> plus $0.30 per hour after 12 weeks
> plus $0.25 per hour after 36 weeks
> plus $0.25 per hour each 6 months thereafter)

Hourly Wage	×	Hours per Week	×	Weeks per Year	=	Yearly gross earnings before taxes
$4.70	×	40	×	4	=	$ 752.00 (first 4)
$5.00	×	40	×	12	=	$ 2,400.00 (after 12)
$5.25	×	40	×	36	=	$ 7,560.00 (after 36)
				52		$10,712.00

Working for Company B would give you $312.00 more the first year alone.

Knowing the opportunity for raises will make your decision regarding employment data-based . . . and, therefore, more valid.

INTERVIEW INFORMATION TOOL

WHAT YOU MUST KNOW **DURING** THE INTERVIEW:

Jobs Discussed During the Interview: *CLERK·TYPIST LEVEL II (SALES DEPT)*

Job Duties: *TYPING, PHONES, FILING, RESEARCH, REPORTS*

Rate of Pay: *$5.50 PER HOUR*

Raises/Pay/Increases: *90 DAY PROBATION (50¢ RAISE EVERY 6 MOS)*

Fringe Benefits: *MEDICAL, DENTAL, PROFIT SHARING AFTER 1 YEAR*

FRINGE BENEFITS:

An hourly rate of $5.00 with all medical, dental, and vacation paid, along with profit sharing, etc., is a much better deal than a company that pays $5.50 per hour with no benefits.

Average employee benefit packages range to about 20% of the salary. That is, at the rate of $5.00 per hour, company-paid benefits increase the pay by 20% (a $1.00 increase). To say this a different way . . . the rate of pay at $5.00 per hour with benefits (add 20%) is really $6.00 per hour.

Benefits can include medical/dental insurance, vacation pay, profit sharing, free subscriptions to wholesale outlets or entertainment centers, paid education programs, etc. The list can go on and on depending on the company.

This is important to consider BEFORE you accept the final offer.

INTERVIEW INFORMATION TOOL

WHAT YOU MUST KNOW **DURING** THE INTERVIEW:

Jobs Discussed During the Interview: _CLERK TYPIST LEVEL II (SALES DEPT)_

Job Duties: _TYPING, PHONES, FILING, RESEARCH, REPORTS)_

Rate of Pay: _$5.50 PER HOUR_

Raises/Pay/Increases: _90 DAY PROBATION (50¢ RAISE EVERY 6 MOS)_

Fringe Benefits: _MEDICAL, DENTAL, PROFIT SHARING AFTER 1 YEAR_

Opportunities for Advancement: _YES - COMPANY EXPANDING_

OPPORTUNITIES FOR ADVANCEMENT:

If you have career ambitions, the opportunity for advancement should be known prior to employment acceptance. A "dead end job" may be acceptable if you understand that those are the conditions. However, if you aspire to new heights, a job without advancement opportunities will be frustrating!

INTERVIEW INFORMATION TOOL

WHAT YOU MUST KNOW **DURING** THE INTERVIEW:

Jobs Discussed During the Interview: _CLERK TYPIST·LEVEL II (SALES DEPT)_

Job Duties: _TYPING, PHONES, FILING, RESEARCH, REPORTS_

Rate of Pay: _$5.50 PER HOUR_

Raises/Pay/Increases: _90 DAY PROBATION (50¢ RAISE EVERY 6 MOS)_

Fringe Benefits: _MEDICAL, DENTAL, PROFIT SHARING AFTER 1 YEAR_

Opportunities for Advancement: _YES- COMPANY EXPANDING_

On-The-Job Training: **YES - COMPANY PAID**

ON-THE-JOB TRAINING:

While most companies require entry level skills (basic skills needed to perform job duties), some firms still train their employees or pay for their training. If you intend to go to college or evening school while working, this information may be financially advantageous to you.

Some companies have training programs available on the job site.

If you can learn while you earn, you have a tremendous advantage over just earning.

INTERVIEW INFORMATION TOOL

WHAT YOU MUST KNOW **DURING** THE INTERVIEW:

Jobs Discussed During the Interview: _CLERK TYPIST·LEVEL II (SALES DEPT)_

Job Duties: _TYPING, PHONES, FILING, RESEARCH, REPORTS_

Rate of Pay: _$5.50 PER HOUR_

Raises/Pay/Increases: _90 DAY PROBATION (50¢ RAISE EVERY 6 MOS)_

Fringe Benefits: _MEDICAL, DENTAL, PROFIT SHARING AFTER 1 YR_

Opportunities for Advancement: _YES - COMPANY EXPANDING_

On-The-Job Training: _YES - COMPANY PAID_

Work Schedule: _8 AM - 4 PM_

Breaks: _TWO - 15 MINUTE_   Lunch: _½ HOUR_

WORK SCHEDULE/BREAKS/LUNCH:

When you are invited to "come to work tomorrow," it is embarrassing to show up at 8:00 a.m. when work began at 7:30 a.m.

Find out the work schedule including beginning and ending shift, break, and lunch times.

Record them for later reference when comparing jobs.

INTERVIEW INFORMATION TOOL

WHAT YOU MUST ASK **DURING** THE INTERVIEW:

Jobs Discussed During the Interview: *CLERK TYPIST LEVEL II (SALES DEPT)*

Job Duties: *TYPING, PHONES, FILING, RESEARCH, REPORTS*

Rate of Pay: *$5.50 PER HOUR*

Raises/Pay/Increases: *90 DAY PROBATION (50¢ RAISE EVERY 6 MOS)*

Fringe Benefits: *MEDICAL, DENTAL, PROFIT SHARING AFTER 1 YR*

Opportunities for Advancement: *YES — COMPANY EXPANDING*

On-The-Job Training: *YES — COMPANY PAID*

Work Schedule: *8 AM — 4 PM*

Breaks: *TWO — 15 MINUTE*   Lunch: *½ HOUR*

When Will I Know? *TOMORROW*

WHEN WILL I KNOW:

Before you terminate the interview, find out when you will know whether or not you will be offered the job. Be sure to restate your interest in the job.

No matter how promising the interview, DO NOT go home and sit by the phone, but continue your job search and daily call your message phone (a relative, neighbor, friend, etc. who is usually home). Most companies will not call to tell you that you were not hired.

INTERVIEW INFORMATION TOOL

WHAT YOU MUST ASK **DURING** THE INTERVIEW:

Jobs Discussed During the Interview: _CLERK·TYPIST LEVEL II (SALES DEPT)_

Job Duties: _TYPING, PHONES, FILING, RESEARCH, REPORTS_

Rate of Pay: _$5.50 PER HOUR_

Raises/Pay/Increases: _90 DAY PROBATION (50¢ RAISE EVERY 6 MOS)_

Fringe Benefits: _MEDICAL, DENTAL, PROFIT SHARING AFTER 1 YEAR_

Opportunities for Advancement: _YES – COMPANY EXPANDING_

On-The-Job Training: _YES–COMPANY PAID_

Work Schedule: _8 AM – 4 PM_

Breaks: _TWO – 15 MINUTE_   Lunch: _1/2 HOUR_

When Will I Know? _TOMORROW_

May I Call You? _YES_ When? _10·22·81 AT 2:30 PM_

MAY I CALL YOU? WHEN?

If the interviewer is vague about the actual hiring, ask him or her, "May I call you?" If the answer is yes, then inquire, "When?"

DO NOT call back more than once a week. However, if you are given a date and time, be sure to call back on that given date and time!

INTERVIEW INFORMATION TOOL

WHAT YOU MUST ASK **DURING** THE INTERVIEW:

Jobs Discussed During the Interview: _CLERK TYPIST·LEVEL II (SALES DEPT)_

Job Duties: _TYPING, PHONES, FILING, RESEARCH, REPORTS_

Rate of Pay: _$5.50 PER HOUR_

Raises/Pay/Increases: _90 DAY PROBATION (50¢ RAISE EVERY 6 MOS)_

Fringe Benefits: _MEDICAL, DENTAL, PROFIT SHARING AFTER 1 YR_

Opportunities for Advancement: _YES— COMPANY EXPANDING_

On-The-Job Training: _YES—COMPANY PAID_

Work Schedule: _8 AM– 4 PM_

Breaks: _TWO–15 MINUTE_   Lunch: _1/2 HOUR_

When Will I Know? _TOMORROW_

May I Call You? _YES_   When? _10·22·81 AT 2:30 PM_

THANK YOU. ✓

THANK YOU:

Be sure to thank the person for the interview no matter how it went. That company has just expended dollars relative to man hours on you and a sincere verbal, "Thank you" is appreciated.

You may also wish to send the interviewer a thank-you note at a later date. This action shows how considerate you are while reminding the interviewer that you are still very interested. (See Section entitled POST INTERVIEW TECHNIQUES: Thank-You Notes, page 192, for more details.)

INTERVIEW INFORMATION TOOL

WHAT YOU MUST ASK **DURING** THE INTERVIEW:

Jobs Discussed During the Interview: _CLERK· TYPIST LEVEL II (SALES DEPT)_

Job Duties: _TYPING, PHONES, FILING, RESEARCH, REPORTS_

Rate of Pay: _$5.50 PER HOUR_

Raises/Pay/Increases: _90 DAY PROBATION (50¢ RAISE EVERY 6 MOS)_

Fringe Benefits: _MEDICAL, DENTAL, PROFIT SHARING AFTER 1 YEAR_

Opportunities for Advancement: _YES—COMPANY EXPANDING_

On-The-Job Training: _YES— COMPANY PAID_

Work Schedule: _8 AM— 4 PM_

Breaks: _TWO- 15 MINUTE_   Lunch: _½ HOUR_

When Will I Know? _TOMORROW!_

May I Call You? _✓_   When? _10·22·81 AT 2:30 PM_

THANK YOU. ✓

Notes: _MRS BROWN IS PERSONNEL SECRETARY_
WORD PROCESSING SYSTEM

NOTES:

After you leave, record any additional information of importance to you.

You can also record additional information relative to the job you are applying for.

> ## KEY CONCEPT
>
> **S** Plan to arrive early for your interview and relax. Be friendly with the secretary and use appropriate courtesies with the interviewer. Sit up straight, smile, and respond to the interviewer's questions in a positive manner. Ask the questions listed on the bottom half of the INTERVIEW INFORMATION TOOL: WHAT YOU MUST ASK **DURING** THE INTERVIEW (example on page 175). Record the answers so you can make a rational decision regarding employment.
>
> Blank copies of the INTERVIEW INFORMATION TOOL are provided at the back of this book starting on page 249.

INTERVIEW INFORMATION TOOL

WHAT YOU MUST KNOW **BEFORE** THE INTERVIEW:

Day: **WEDNESDAY**   Date: **OCT 21**   Time: **9:00 AM**

Company Name: **WE·CAN· DO MANUFACTURING CO**

Address: **341 ROSEWOOD   S.D.**

Interviewer's Name: **MR JONES**   Title: **PERSONNEL DIRECTOR**

Room Number: **MAIN PERS OFC** Phone Number: **222-7644** Extension: **98**

Transportation: **CAR**   Parking: **VISITORS LOT # 1**

Major Facts About the Company: **ALUMINUM CAN MANUFACTURERS**
DOING BUSINESS FOR 20 YEARS - 2000 EMPLOYEES

Job You Want at This Company: **CLERK· TYPIST**

WHAT YOU MUST ASK **DURING** THE INTERVIEW:

Jobs Discussed During the Interview: **CLERK TYPIST LEVEL II (SALES DEPT)**

Job Duties: **TYPING, PHONES, FILING, RESEARCH, REPORTS**

Rate of Pay: **$5.50 PER HOUR**

Raises/Pay/Increases: **90 DAY PROBATION (50¢ RAISE EVERY 6 MOS)**

Fringe Benefits: **MEDICAL, DENTAL, PROFIT SHARING AFTER 1 YEAR**

Opportunities for Advancement: **YES- COMPANY EXPANDING**

On-The-Job Training: **YES—COMPANY PAID**

Work Schedule: **8AM— 4 PM**

Breaks: **TWO- 15 MINUTE**   Lunch: **½ HOUR**

When Will I Know? **TOMORROW**

May I Call You? **YES**   When? **10·22·81 AT 2:30 PM**

THANK YOU. ✔

Notes: **MRS BROWN IS PERSONNEL SECRETARY**
WORD PROCESSING SYSTEM

INTERVIEW DRAMATIZATION

This section is a dialogue of a typical interview written in the same manner as a screenplay or drama. The drama players are the personnel office workers and the person applying for employment.

The sequence illustrates the way it should be done . . . not necessarily the way it always is!

"Now Or Never"

A Screenplay by Lawrence E. Barlow, M.A.

SETTING:

We-Can-Do Manufacturing Company —
Main Personnel Office

CAST:

Mickey Moore (Applicant): A mild-mannered individual desiring work.

Mr. Jones (Interviewer): A nice man who wants to hire the best qualified people for the company.

Mrs. Brown (Secretary): The Personnel Secretary who wants to keep everybody happy.

ENTER: Mickey Moore (dressed in a gray color-coordinated jacket, blouse, and skirt, low heels, wearing appropriate make-up and expressing a sincere smile). Mickey approaches Mrs. Brown, who is behind her desk in the Personnel Office.

Mickey: "Good Morning! I have skills as a clerk-typist and would like to apply for a position in your company." (taking note of Mrs. Brown's desk nameplate)

Mrs. Brown: "We have no advertised openings at the present time."

(pause)

Mickey: "May I fill out an application?"

Mrs. Brown: "Certainly." (handing Mickey an application) "Fill this out and return it to me."

Mickey: "Thank you very much." (expressing gratitude and another gentle smile)

(Mickey takes a seat, gets out her erasable ink pen, and proceeds to copy all the information previously researched and recorded on her APPLICATION INFORMATION TOOL.)

SEVEN MINUTES LATER: Mickey double-checks her application, making sure all blanks are filled in appropriately. She then proceeds to return her application to Mrs. Brown, who has her back to Mickey.

Mickey: "Excuse me, Mrs. Brown, may I give you my application?"

Mrs. Brown: "Oh! Yes. Do you have it completed already?" (impressed with Mickey's speed and accuracy)

Mickey: "I have filled in all the blanks . . . may I attach a copy of my resume?"

Mrs. Brown: (while reading the legible application with much interest) "Yes, an attached resume is always welcome. Have a seat, please. I would like to show your application and resume to Mr. Jones, our Personnel Director."

EXIT: Mrs. Brown, still reading the resume and application.

[Mickey realizes there is an interview possibility. She therefore takes out her INTERVIEW INFORMATION TOOL, fills in the name of the interviewer (Mr. Jones), and notes that Mrs. Brown is the Personnel Secretary.] (See example on page 190.)

(Mickey sits down and realizes that she is nervous — sweaty hands, cold shivers . . . "Oh my!" she says to herself. "It is NOW or NEVER!" She recalls from her treasured *THE JOB-SEEKERS' BIBLE* that if she rubbed her throat her voice would not fail. Rubbing her hands together seems to burn off anxiety and breathing deeply provides enough oxygen. She flexes her upper leg muscles, smiles, and feels much better.)

ENTER: Mrs. Brown:

Mrs. Brown: "Ms. Moore, Mr. Jones has read your application and resume. He would like to chat with you. Do you have some free time now?"

Mickey: "Yes I do and I would like to talk . . . but, please call me Mickey." (with a sincere smile)

Mrs. Brown: "Certainly, Mickey . . . please come with me."

(As Mickey follows Mrs. Brown into Mr. Jones' office, she thinks how glad she is to be prepared . . . extra resume copies, *THE JOB-SEEKERS' BIBLE,* and clothes that make her feel good . . . she is ready!)

Mrs. Brown: "Mr. Jones, I would like to introduce Ms. Moore," (pausing and smiling) "that is, Mickey Moore. Mickey, this is Mr. Jones, our Personnel Director."

Mickey: "It is a pleasure to meet you, Mr. Jones." (as she fixes his name in her mind and extends her hand for a firm handshake)

Mr. Jones: (as he shakes her hand and invites Mickey to take a seat) "It is nice to have you come in today." (he continues in light conversation) "What is the weather like out there?"

Mickey: "It is a beautiful day, and I am glad to be here . . . even though I am a bit nervous."

Mr. Jones: (in a reassuring manner) "Don't be
              nervous, Mickey. I see you have skills
              as a clerk-typist. How did you come by
              those skills?"

Mickey: "I took a business class in high school
              which I really enjoyed. I went to V.C.
              Business School and then to work. As
              you can see by my resume, I have good
              skills." (not bragging, but confident)
              "But, more than that, I enjoy the
              work."

Mr. Jones: "Why do you want to work for
              We-Can-Do?"

Mickey: (glad she knew something about the
              company) "Your company has a good
              reputation and I like your product line.
              I am impressed by the wage scale and I
              live close by."

Mr. Jones: "Briefly, tell me about yourself."

Mickey: (glad she is ready for this one!) "I am
              even-tempered, learn quickly, and work
              hard. I enjoy office work, but also enjoy
              weekends at the beach."

Mr. Jones: "How do you resolve your differences with people, Mickey? That is, your arguments with people?"

Mickey: (aware of the trick question) "Oh, I never allow my differences to turn into arguments. I am quite easygoing and enjoy most people."

Mr. Jones: "Mickey, an unadvertised opening exists . . . " (as he lights a cigarette) "Oh, excuse me, would you like a cigarette?"

Mickey: [thinking to herself that she surely could use one now, but remembering *THE JOB-SEEKERS' BIBLE* (THE INTERVIEW chapter) mentioning that if she smoked during an interview she probably would not be hired. Smiling at her recall ability, she says . . .] "No, thank you. You are very kind to ask, But, about the opening . . ."

Mr. Jones: "Oh, yes, there is an unadvertised opening . . . an employee is being transferred one month early and I was just notified. Would you be interested in a Level II Clerk-Typist position?"

Mickey: "I am interested, but could you give me more details?"

Mr. Jones: "Sure, what would you like to know?"

Mickey: [as she grasps her favorite pen and prepares to write on the bottom half of her INTERVIEW INFORMATION TOOL) (Refer to example on page 190.) "Is it all right to take notes?"

Mr. Jones: "Certainly." (impressed that what he has to say is noteworthy)

Mickey: "Mr. Jones, what are the job duties?"

Mr. Jones: "Clerk-Typist Level II for our Sales Department consists of typing, answering phones, filing, light research, and reports."

Mickey: (while jotting down the information on the bottom half of the INTERVIEW INFORMATION TOOL, Mickey continues . . .) "What is the rate of pay, probationary period, and could you describe fringe benefits?" (Mickey is glad to have the reminders because Mr. Jones really seems impressed)

Mr. Jones: "The pay scale will be $5.50 per hour
              for a 90-day probationary period. After
              90 days you will get a wage review and
              if favorable, your wages will be in-
              creased 50¢ per hour. Wage reviews are
              every six months with at least a 50¢-an-
              hour increase. All medical and dental
              are paid. We also have a profit-sharing
              program for employees who have been
              with the company a year or longer."

Mickey: "Is there on-the-job training and oppor-
              tunity for advancement?"

Mr. Jones: (thinking to himself that he is very im-
              pressed with Mickey's thoroughness . . .
              hardly anyone ever asks those important
              questions) "Yes, Mickey, We-Can-Do
              has been in business for 20 years and is
              expanding. We have 2,000 employees
              and advancement is available. Upgraded/
              advanced persons are trained on-the-job
              by the company and if you attend out-
              side training courses pertinent to your
              work, the company will pay.

(Mickey proceeds to write the information on her IN-
TERVIEW INFORMATION TOOL bottom section as
well as the major facts on the top section.) (Refer to
example on page 190.)

Mickey: "What hours would I work and how
                 long is the lunch hour?"

Mr. Jones: "You will work from 8:00 a.m. to
                 4:30 p.m. Monday through Friday with
                 two 15-minute breaks and a half hour
                 for lunch."

Mickey: "When would I know if I have a chance
                 for the position?"

Mr. Jones: "I will present your resume and applica-
                 tion to the head of the Sales Depart-
                 ment later today."

Mickey: "May I call you regarding the outcome
                 of that meeting?"

Mr. Jones: "Yes, that would be convenient."

Mickey: "What time would be most
               convenient?"

Mr. Jones: "Tomorrow at 2:30 p.m. would be fine.
               My phone number is 222-7644, Exten-
               sion 98. Is there anything else I can
               answer for you?"

(Mickey proceeds to record the telephone number in the
appropriate place on the top section of the INTER-
VIEW INFORMATION TOOL.) (Refer to example on
page 190.)

Mickey: "Thank you, Mr. Jones, but I think
               that is everything. Do you have any
               more questions?"

Mr. Jones: "No, Mickey, but it has been a pleasure
               talking to you. You are well-prepared."

Mickey: (while rising, extending her hand, and
               smiling) "Thank you for your time and
               effort. I appreciate it and look forward
               to talking with you tomorrow."

(Mickey smiles and exits.)

Mickey: "Mrs. Brown, thank you for your con-
                cern today. I will call back tomorrow."

Mrs. Brown: "Have a good day, Mickey. I am glad
                you came in today."

(Mickey smiles and exits, confident she did everything
in her power to convince Mr. Jones that she is the best
person for the job.)

SCENE: 2:30 p.m. the following day. Mickey has just dialed the We-Can-Do Manufacturing Company.

Mickey: "Hello, this is Mickey Moore. Is
                 Mr. Jones in? He wanted me to call him
                 at this time."

Mrs. Brown: "Hello, Mickey. I'll get him for you."

Mr. Jones: "Hello, Mickey, how are you today?"

Mickey: "Just fine, thank you. I called to see if
                 that job we discussed yesterday is still
                 open."

Mr. Jones: "That depends on you, Mickey. If you
                 would accept the conditions we dis-
                 cussed, I would like to hire you."

Mickey: (with a deep feeling of satisfaction)
                 "I have seriously considered the matter
                 since yesterday, and I accept. When do
                 I begin?"

          THE BEGINNING.

KEY CONCEPT

This Mock Interview is a bit exaggerated, but does compare to a real one. Your interview is a NOW or NEVER situation. If you are prepared . . . that is, know yourself and know how to use the TOOLS and TECHNIQUES in this book . . . you will get the job you want. If you have read this book and use it during your job search, you will be prepared much better than your competition.

The INTERVIEW INFORMATION TOOL on page 190 illustrates how the TOOL looks after Mickey's entire interview. Remember, the entire INTERVIEW INFORMATION TOOL should be complete by the end of the interview so you will have accurate and adequate data with which to make a decision. If you are offered employment by two different companies on the same day, the INTERVIEW INFORMATION TOOL is an excellent comparison device. If you are called two weeks after the interview and offered a position, you can easily review all aspects of the job without asking embarrasing questions which were already covered in the initial interview.

The INTERVIEW INFORMATION TOOL is a very important key to your success.

INTERVIEW INFORMATION TOOL

WHAT YOU MUST KNOW **BEFORE** THE INTERVIEW:

Day: **WEDNESDAY**   Date: **OCT 21**   Time: **9:00 AM**

Company Name: **WE·CAN·DO MFG CO**

Address: **341 ROSEWOOD   S.D.**

Interviewer's Name: **MR JONES**   Title: **PERSONNEL DIRECTOR**

Room Number: **MAIN PERS OFC** Phone Number: **222-7644**   Extension: **98**

Transportation: **CAR**   Parking: **VISITORS LOT # 1**

Major Facts About the Company: **ALUMINUM CAN MANUFACTURERS**
DOING BUSINESS FOR 20 YEARS · 2000 EMPLOYEES

Job You Want at This Company: **CLERK· TYPIST**

WHAT YOU MUST ASK **DURING** THE INTERVIEW:

Jobs Discussed During the Interview: **CLERK·TYPIST LEVEL II (SALES DEPT)**

Job Duties: **TYPING, PHONES, FILING, RESEARCH, REPORTS**

Rate of Pay: **$5.50 PER HOUR**

Raises/Pay/Increases: **90 DAY PROBATION (50¢ RAISE EVERY 6 MOS)**

Fringe Benefits: **MEDICAL, DENTAL, PROFIT SHARING AFTER 1 YEAR**

Opportunities for Advancement: **YES – COMPANY EXPANDING**

On-The-Job Training: **YES – COMPANY PAID**

Work Schedule: **8 AM – 4 PM**

Breaks: **TWO - 15 MINUTE**   Lunch: **½ HOUR**

When Will I Know? **TOMORROW**

May I Call You? **YES**   When? **10·22·81 AT 2:30 PM**

THANK YOU. **✓**

Notes: **MRS BROWN IS PERSONNEL SECRETARY**
WORD PROCESSING SYSTEM

WHAT TO BRING

☐ Bring this book (after you have read it, understood it, and filled in all the necessary TOOLS).

☐ Have the following TOOLS and TECHNIQUES in order:

☐ 1. YOUR BODY —

in appropriate dress (Chapter 7)

☐ 2. APPLICATION INFORMATION TOOL —

(Chapter 5)

☐ 3. RESUME —

if you have one (six copies) (Chapter 9)

☐ 4. LETTERS OF RECOMMENDATION —

if you have them (photocopies are acceptable) (Chapter 10)

☐ 5. INTERVIEW INFORMATION TOOL —

(Chapter 8)

☐ 6. PENS —

two with erasable ink

☐ 7. PENCILS —

two with erasers

☐ 8. CONFIDENCE —

(for if you have read this book, you are well prepared!)

POST-INTERVIEW TECHNIQUES
Thank-You Notes

After you have left the interview, it is perfectly acceptable (and to your advantage) to send the interviewer a typed or handwritten thank-you note.

Companies expend time and effort interviewing and appreciation of this fact shows your sincerity and awareness. Business time and effort equals money.

An example of a short note of appreciation follows:

Most personnel officers/interviewers never receive thank-you notes although it is perfectly acceptable. Why not be one of the few to be thoughtful enough to send one? Besides that, it has other less obvious implications. The thank-you note reminds the interviewer of you in a pleasant and sincere manner. This reminder can be the key to job procurement even if your interview was not. Remember, they HIRE YOU BECAUSE THEY LIKE YOU and a sincere, brief thank-you note will help them to like you.

Telephone Follow-Up

If, after two or three days you have not heard from the company where you interviewed, it is reasonable to contact the person who interviewed you. The telephone is an excellent TOOL. Remember . . . at the end of the interview when you asked if you could call back, the interviewer responded that inquiry calls were acceptable. Check your INTERVIEW INFORMATION TOOL to see if a date and time to call back were given. Also check your PHONE SEARCH TOOL (Chapter 6) to see if it is time to call back for possible openings.

Dial the phone and with CONFIDENCE and POISE say:

"Hello, may I please speak to _____ at extension _____?" (always have complete reference and contact information exact)

(after connection has been made) "Hello,
_____, this is _____
and I am calling regarding the job we discussed
during our interview last Friday morning." (pause
and allow the interviewer time to respond, then
spontaneously finish your conversation)

If notified you were hired, collect pertinent information so you can begin work. If you were not hired, respond in the following manner:

"I understand the situation and again, thank you
for your time and consideration. Is it all right if I
call you back on a weekly basis regarding future
openings?"

Don't lose your contact with people . . . especially
those who could hire you. Call back weekly, but no more
often than that. Make your once-a-week call-backs
short and sweet . . . but make them. Potential employers
admire persistence (once a week) but dislike pestering
(more than once a week).

> ## — KEY CONCEPT —
>
> Following-up an interview with a thank-you note helps the interviewer remember you in a pleasant manner. Telephone calls and revisits are acceptable if done in moderation. Keep in contact with potential employers.

SUMMARY

The interview is a job-matching process intended to identify an appropriate job for an appropriate employee. It can be compared to a screenplay where the business of hiring is acted out. Most interviews are similar and most questions can be anticipated.

You should arrive early, relax, and be friendly to the secretary. Be sure to bring appropriate pens, pencils, confidence, and the TECHNIQUES and TOOLS given in *THE JOB-SEEKERS' BIBLE.* Be courteous, keep good eye contact, and shake hands when appropriate. Do not chew gum or smoke.

The INTERVIEW INFORMATION TOOL is your most important asset before and during the interview. The top half of the INTERVIEW INFORMATION TOOL (WHAT YOU MUST KNOW **BEFORE** THE INTERVIEW) is filled in when the interview is set up. The bottom half of the INTERVIEW INFORMATION TOOL (WHAT YOU MUST ASK **DURING** THE IN-TERVIEW) is filled in during the interview. Use this TOOL to record the information needed to make a sound decision regarding employment. Blank copies of the INTERVIEW INFORMATION TOOL are pro-vided at the end of the book on page 249.

Thank-you notes and follow-up phone calls are courtesies that should be extended

CHAPTER 9
You In Print

RESUMES

RESUME TOOL

COVER LETTERS

You In Print

RESUMES

WHAT IS A RESUME?

A resume (sometimes referred to as a Personal Data Sheet) is a technically written description of a person's vocational skills, training, and work experience in less than two pages (see examples starting on page 216).

WHY A RESUME?

A resume does the following things for you:

1. A resume helps you, the job-seeker, organize your skills, training, experience, background data, and other job-related information.
2. A resume can be handed to a busy potential employer so that your qualifications can be quickly assessed. It makes the potential employer's job easier, and that is a plus factor for YOU.
3. A resume shows the potential employer that you are just a little bit more prepared. Only one in seven job-seekers has a resume.
4. A resume, when printed on quality 20-pound bond paper and attached to an employment application, stands erect in the file while the other employment applications go limp. Attention is drawn to the thicker, more erect file.

5. A resume serves as an advertisement brochure and can be given to friends, relatives, social groups, church groups, professional/trade associations, and placement offices so their contacts can read all about you. You never know who is looking for a good employee.

WHO CAN MAKE A RESUME?

Private companies offering resume services charge anywhere from $25 to $250. You, by following the simple TECHNIQUES in this chapter, can make your own resume.

SHOULD A RESUME BE TYPEWRITTEN?

YES! Always type a resume. Proofread the finished product carefully since it must be free from all errors.

WHAT ABOUT COPIES?

A quality copy of your flawless original resume is perfectly acceptable. Remember to keep your original in a safe place for future copies as needed. A quality 20-pound bond paper from an Instant Print Shop is excellent. Colored paper is acceptable in the subtle shades of off-white, ivory, or tan.

RESUME TOOL

HOW TO DEVELOP YOUR OWN RESUME

1. Review the example resumes at the end of this section starting on page 216. Select the model that is most appropriate to your background. Imitate the "model" but use your own skills, experience, etc. to develop your resume.

2. Fill in the blank RESUME TOOL, located on page 250, according to the step-by-step guidelines starting on page 202. Refer to the RESUME POWER WORDS on page 211 if you need help with impact word selection. An example of a completed RESUME TOOL has been provided on page 213.

3. Type your resume from the information on the RESUME TOOL paying close attention to spacing and categories. If you do not type, have someone type it for you.

4. Proofread your typed copy carefully and/or have a friend proofread it.

5. Take the finished typed and proofread copy to an Instant Printer where copy quality is high and prices are reasonable.

6. Distribute your resume everywhere you can . . . neighbors, relatives, ministers, priests, friends . . . anyone who may pass it on to a potential employer.

RESUME TOOL

NAME: _CAROLYN V. MILLER_

NAME:

Do not use Ms. in front of your first name for it implies "Women's Libber" and some employers might not care for assertive females.

Do not use Mrs. in front of your first name for it implies "children" and many employers are concerned about extensive absenteeism because of them.

Do not use Miss in front of your first name because some employers might not want an "irresponsible" single girl.

Do not use Mr. in front of your first name because some employers may think you have a "high and mighty" attitude.

Just use your first name, middle initial, and last name.

RESUME TOOL

NAME: _CAROLYN V. MILLER_

ADDRESS: _111 WOOD WAY, #10 SAN DIEGO, CA. 92010_

ADDRESS:

List your address including your house number, apartment letter or number, or your Post Office Box number. Spell out all street, city, and state names. The correct zip code should also be included.

RESUME TOOL

NAME: _CAROLYN V. MILLER_

ADDRESS: _111 WOOD WAY, #10_

TELEPHONE NUMBER: _714 561-0090_

MESSAGE NUMBER: _714 440-2542_

TELEPHONE/MESSAGE NUMBERS:

The TELEPHONE NUMBER should be your home phone number.

The MESSAGE NUMBER should be a number where someone responsible can take a message for you . . . a reliable friend, a relative, en elderly neighbor, or an answering service.

Area codes should be included.

RESUME TOOL

NAME: *CAROLYN V. MILLER*

ADDRESS: *III WOOD WAY, #10, SAN DIEGO CA 92010*

TELEPHONE NUMBER: *714 561-0090*

MESSAGE NUMBER: *714 440-2542*

SKILLS: *TYPING (60 WORDS PER MINUTE), DICTAPHONE TRANSCRIPTION, FILING, MAIL, SWITCHBOARD, RECEPTIONIST, PUBLIC RELATIONS*

SKILLS:

List the skills you have and be brief. Specific terms such as arc welding, lathe/mill machine operation, accounts payable/receivable, D-6 dozer operator are examples of skills.

Any skill you perform should be listed. A company hires you because they like you and because they can use your skills.

RESUME TOOL

NAME: _CAROLYN V. MILLER_

ADDRESS: _III WOOD WAY #10 SAN DIEGO, CA 92010_

TELEPHONE NUMBER: _714 561-0090_

MESSAGE NUMBER: _714 440-2542_

SKILLS: _TYPING, (60 WORDS PER MINUTE) DICTAPHONE_
TRANSCRIPTION, FILING, MAIL, SWITCHBOARD, RECEPTION-
IST, PUBLIC RELATIONS

EXPERIENCE:

1983 to PRES _JET AERONAUTICAL CO_
Company Name

EL CAJON, CA 92022
City   State   Zip

ENGINEERING SECRETARY
Your Title

GENERAL OFFICE: TECHNICAL PROPOSALS
Your Responsibilities and/or duties

MEETING MINUTES,
SERVICE/WORK ORDERS
FILING SYSTEM

EXPERIENCE:

1. List most recent experience first.
2. Paid experience is desired BUT volunteer experience can be listed.
3. Be brief but use no abbreviations.
4. Avoid listing experience of less than two months.
5. Use action words (see RESUME POWER WORDS on page 211.)
6. List no more than six jobs under EXPERIENCE.

EDUCATION: **NEEDLES COMMUNITY COLLEGE**
(Most recent first) School Name
              LA MESA,   CA
              City   State
              ASSOCIATE IN ARTS DEGREE: BUS. ADM.
              Degree — Certificate — Courses — Units — Workshops, etc.
              1984
              Year Attended
              (Graduated)

              NEEDMORE ADULT SCHOOL S.D.CA
              School Name   City State
              GENERAL SECRETARIAL CERTIFICATE
              Degree — Certificate — Courses — Units — Workshops, etc.
              1981
              Year Attended
              (Graduated)

              MORTON COMMUNITY HS S.D CA
              School Name   City State
              GRADUATE
              Degree — Certificate — Courses — Units — Workshops, etc.
              1979
              Year Attended
              (Graduated)

EDUCATION:

EDUCATION listings should begin with the school last attended. Be brief but describe the course activities and make yourself look as positive as possible. If you graduated, insert GRADUATE. If you did not graduate, insert the number of units or credits received or the number of hours attended. SKILLS and EXPERIENCE are most impressive, of primary importance to the prospective employer, and are usually listed before EDUCATION.

EDUCATION:
(Most recent first)

NEEDLES COMMUNITY COLLEGE
School Name

LA MESA   CA
City   State

ASSOCIATE IN ARTS DEGREE: BUS ADM
Degree — Certificate — Courses — Units — Workshops, etc.

1984
Year Attended
(Graduated)

NEEDMORE ADULT SCHOOL
School Name

SAN DIEGO,   CA
City   State

GENERAL SECRETARIAL CERTIFICATE
Degree — Certificate — Courses — Units — Workshops, etc.

1981
Year Attended
(Graduated)

MORTON COMMUNITY HIGH SCHOOL
School Name

SAN DIEGO   CA
City   State

GRADUATE
Degree — Certificate — Courses — Units — Workshops, etc.

1979
Year Attended
(Graduated)

ACHIEVEMENTS:
(Optional)

NATIONAL SECRETARIES ASSN
SAN DIEGO CHAPTER;
SECRETARY OF THE YEAR
AWARD, 1982

ACHIEVEMENTS:

This is your opportunity to list your accomplishments and honors received at work, in the community, and/or during your education. Be brief, stating the organization, the award and/or accomplishment, and the year received.

EDUCATION: NEEDLES COMMUNITY COLLEGE
(Most recent first) School Name
               LA MESA   CA
               City   State
               ASSOCIATE OF ARTS DEGREE: BUS AD.
               Degree — Certificate — Courses — Units — Workshops, etc.
               1984
               Year Attended
               (Graduated)

               NEEDMORE ADULT SCHOOL
               School Name
               SAN DIEGO   CA
               City   State
               GENERAL SECRETARIAL CERTIFICATE
               Degree — Certificate — Courses — Units — Workshops, etc.
               1981
               Year Attended
               (Graduated)

               MORTON COMMUNITY HIGH SCHOOL
               School Name
               SAN DIEGO   CA
               City   State
               GRADUATE
               Degree — Certificate — Courses — Units — Workshops, etc.
               1979
               Year Attended
               (Graduated)

ACHIEVEMENTS: NATIONAL SECRETARIES ASSN-
(Optional)   SAN DIEGO CHAPTER: SECRETARY
               OF THE YEAR AWARD, 1982

Hobbies: OIL PAINTING,
(Optional —   INTERIOR DECORATING,
depending on
room available) TENNIS

HOBBIES:

Any activity you do is indicative of your skills, so
be sure to mention any if there is room on your resume.
A good hobby illustrates your leisure time productivity.

ACHIEVEMENTS: NATIONAL SECRETARIES ASSN,
(Optional) SAN DIEGO CHAPTER;
SECRETARY OF THE YEAR
AWARD, 1978

Hobbies: OIL PAINTING
(Optional — INTERIOR DECORATING
depending on
room available) TENNIS

REFERENCES: Available upon request

REFERENCES: MS. MARY KAY BROWN
Name
PERSONNEL DIRECTOR
Title
CANCO MANUFACTURING COMPANY
Company Name
123 JEWELL STREET
Address
SAN DIEGO, CA 92010
City   State   Zip
714 461-8111
Area Code   Telephone Number

REFERENCES:

Under the heading of references, you can indicate the phrase, "Available upon request." A separate reference sheet can then be made available to the potential employer upon request or attached to the resume itself as shown on pages 216-217.

References can also be listed on the bottom portion of the resume as per example on page 219.

Verify and confirm each reference before listing them. Use work, school, and/or professional references when possible.

The RESUME TOOL includes spaces for you to record four REFERENCES. You should have at least three.

RESUME POWER WORDS

accomplishments
accountable
activities
adjustment
administration
advised
analysis
analyze
answering
apprentice
area
assessment
assign
assignment
authorized
available

basis
bonded

calculate
calculations
call
carved
catalog
certified
charge
clamps
classification
classifies
clerk
coached
collation
collection
communication
compared
compiled
complete
composed
comprehensive
computing
conducted
conferred
conjunction

construction
consulted
continuous
contracts
control
coordinated
coordination
copies
correspondence
creation
cut
curriculum

daily
decisive
design
designated
detailed
determined
developed
developer
development
directed
directives
dispatching
duties

education
emphasis
employment
established
evaluated
evaluation
examine
examination
expanded
expediting

facilities
fastened
figures
fixed
following
formulated

full
functions
furnished

general
graduate
guidance
guided

handled
hiring
hobbies
honorable

illustrates
implements
include
incorporated
indicated
initiating
innovate
innovative
inserts
in-servicing
inspection
instruct
instruction
intensive
interests
interpreted
interviewed
invented
investigated
involving
issues

justification

leadership
lectured
liaison
licensed
lifted
loaded

maintenance
major
management
member
met
mixed
monitored

negotiations

objectives
operation
opportunity
organizes
orientation
originates
outstanding

participation
periodic
personnel
persuaded
phases
planning
policy
positions
preparation
present
presses
procurement
profits
program
promoted
program
purchase

rank
receiving
receptionist
recommend
recorded
reduced
references

regulates
related
relations
request
research
responsibilities
review
routine

scheduling
scrapes
securing
selected
service
setting
shipping
sketched
sold
solicited
sorts
studied
supervised
supervision
support

task
teaches
techniques
trainee
training
transcription
trims
trouble-shooting

updating

various
vehicles
verifies
volunteer

writes

KEY CONCEPT

The TECHNIQUES given for writing a resume were brief and specific. If your experience and/or education is more complex, you can review some of the example resumes starting on page 216, and formulate your own in a similar manner.

Keep in mind the following points:

1. PERFECTLY TYPED: The resume reflects YOU IN PRINT and mistakes make you look unqualified.

2. TWO-PAGE MAXIMUM LENGTH: Busy business people don't have time to read long resumes and won't. If it is too long it will be discarded. A one-page resume is ideal.

3. IMPRESSIVE INFORMATION ON FIRST PAGE: After your name, address, and phone number you must immediately catch the reader's eye . . . encourage them to read on . . . like an advertisement.

4. INVEST IN GOOD COPIES: Go to an Instant Print Shop and have good copies made. A poor copy is a reflection of YOU and will detract from your good impression.

RESUME TOOL

NAME: CAROLYN V. MILLER

ADDRESS: 111 WOOD WAY #10, SAN DIEGO, CA, 92010

TELEPHONE NUMBER: 714 561-0090

MESSAGE NUMBER: 714 440-2542

SKILLS: TYPING (60 WPM) DICTAPHONE TRANSCRIPTION, FILING, MAIL, SWITCHBOARD, RECEPTIONIST, PUBLIC RELATIONS

EXPERIENCE:

1983 to PRES JET AERONAUTICAL COMPANY
Company Name

EL CAJON, CA 92022
City   State   Zip

ENGINEERING SECRETARY
Your Title

GENERAL OFFICE: TECHNICAL
Your Responsibilities and/or duties

PROPOSALS, MEETING MINUTES, SERVICE/WORK ORDERS, FILING SYSTEM

1981 to 1983 PACIFIC INSURANCE CO
Company Name

SAN DIEGO, CA 92011
City   State   Zip

SECRETARY
Your Title

GENERAL OFFICE INCLUDING PHONES
Your Responsibilities and/or duties

TYPING, DICTAPHONE, FILING, LETTER COMPOSITION, POLICY FOLLOW-UP, PUBLIC RELATIONS

EDUCATION: **NEEDLES COMMUNITY COLLEGE**
(Most recent first) School Name
                     LA MESA,   CA
                     City   State
                     ASSOCIATE IN ARTS DEGREE; BUS ADM
                     Degree — Certificate — Courses — Units — Workshops, etc.
                     1984
                     Year Attended
                     (Graduated)

                     NEEDMORE ADULT SCHOOL
                     School Name
                     SAN DIEGO,   CA
                     City   State
                     GENERAL SECRETARIAL CERT.
                     Degree — Certificate — Courses — Units — Workshops, etc.
                     1981
                     Year Attended
                     (Graduated)

                     MORTON COMMUNITY HIGH SCHOOL
                     School Name
                     SAN DIEGO,   CA
                     City   State
                     GRADUATE
                     Degree — Certificate — Courses — Units — Workshops, etc.
                     1979
                     Year Attended
                     (Graduated)

ACHIEVEMENTS: **NATIONAL SECRETARIES ASSN,**
(Optional)   **SAN DIEGO CHAPTER;**
                    SECRETARY OF THE YEAR
                    AWARD, 1982

Hobbies: **OIL PAINTING,**
(Optional —   **INTERIOR DECORATING,**
depending on   **TENNIS**
room available)

REFERENCES: Available upon request

REFERENCES: **MS. MARY KAY BROWN**
Name
PERSONNEL DIRECTOR
Title
CANCO MANUFACTURING COMPANY
Company Name
123 JEWELL ST
Address
SAN DIEGO, CA. 92010
City State Zip
714 461-8111
Area Code Telephone Number

MR. JOSEPH BLUE
Name
OWNER
Title
PACIFIC INSURANCE, INC
Company Name
8917 'G' STREET
Address
SAN DIEGO, CA. 92102
City State Zip
714 442-033
Area Code Telephone Number

MRS. BETTY PAGE
Name
INSTRUCTOR
Title
NEEDMORE ADULT SCHOOL
Company Name
1211 MORRISON STREET
Address
SAN DIEGO, CA 92022
City State Zip
714 579-2810
Area Code Telephone Number

EXAMPLE RESUME:
Work Experience

RESUME

NAME: **CAROLYN V. MILLER**

ADDRESS: 111 Wood Way, #10
                       San Diego, California 92010

TELEPHONE: 561-0090
                       440-2542 (Message Number)

SKILLS: Typing (60 words per minute), dictaphone transcription, filing,
                       mail, switchboard, receptionist, public relations

EXPERIENCE:
1983 - present   Jet Aeronautical Company
                       El Cajon, California 92022
                       ENGINEERING SECRETARY
                       Responsibilities: General office duties including typing
                       technical proposals, meeting minutes; service/work orders;
                       filing system.

1981 - 1983   Pacific Insurance, Inc.
                       San Diego, California 92011
                       SECRETARY
                       Responsibilities: General office including telephones, typing,
                       dictaphone, filing, letter composition, policy follow-up, public
                       relations.

1979 - 1981   Canco Manufacturing Company
                       San Diego, Clifornia 92101
                       RECEPTIONIST
                       Responsibilities: Public relations, switchboard, incoming mail
                       sorting/distribution, typing.

EDUCATION: Needles Community College
                       La Mesa, California
                       Associate in Arts Degree: Business Administration -1984

                       Needmore Adult School
                       San Diego, California
                       General Secretarial Certificate - 1981

                       Morton Community High School
                       San Diego, California
                       Graduate - 1979

ACHIEVEMENTS: National Secretaries Association
                       San Diego Chapter Secretary of the Year Award - 1982

HOBBIES: Oil painting, interior design, tennis

REFERENCES: Available upon request

EXAMPLE REFERENCES

REFERENCES

Ms. Mary Kay Brown
Personnel Director
Canco Manufacturing Company
123 Jewell Street
San Diego, California 92010
(714) 461-8111

Mr. Joseph Blue
Owner
Pacific Insurance, Inc.
8917 "G" Street
San Diego, California 92102
(714) 442-0331

Mrs. Betty Page
Instructor
Needmore Union Adult School
1211 Morrison Street
San Diego, California 92022
(714) 579-2810

EXAMPLE RESUME: Volunteer Experience

PERSONAL DATA SHEET

NAME: **BARBARA L. DAVIS**

ADDRESS: 22 - 152nd Street
Santee, California 92071

TELEPHONE: 579-2771
561-4018 (Message Number)

SKILLS: Public relations, oral/written communications, telephone, typing (45 words per minute), filing, organizing, supervising

EXPERIENCE:

1985 - present
Riverside Elementary School District
Poolside School
Santee, California

SCHOOL ADVISORY COMMITTEE CHAIRPERSON
Conducted bi-monthly meetings for parents/faculty/ administration participants, assisted in planning meeting agendas, attended state wide conferences, written/oral reports, decision making.

PARENT/TEACHERS ASSOCIATION SECRETARY/ PROJECT DIRECTOR
Active member on PTA Board with secretarial skills including minutes, drafting letters to state officials, various fund raising project planner, organizer, and supervisor.

CLASSROOM VOLUNTEER
Volunteered wherever needed on campus.

1984 - 1985
National Little League Association
Santee, California

ADVERTISING/PROMOTION DIRECTOR
Responsible for literature distribution, press releases, auxiliary membership campaign organizer, general assistance.

1984
Mercy General Hospital
San Diego, California

PINK LADY
Responsible for office assistance involving answering telephones, public announcement system operation, typing, errands.

EDUCATION: Lewis Community College — El Cajon, California
15 units of General Education
1984 to present

York Community High School — Madison, Wisconsin
Graduate - 1980

ACHIEVEMENTS: Volunteer Of The Year — City of Santee - 1985
Lewis Community College - Associated Student President -1984

REFERENCES: Available upon request

EXAMPLE RESUME:
High School Graduate

WILLIAM BOYD
65 South Ninth Street
La Mesa, California 92041
560-5543

EMPLOYMENT GOAL:
To develop Journeyman level skills in a trade where I can work with my hands.

SKILLS:
WOODWORKING: Table, hand, radial arm, and scroll saw operation as well as other woodworking related equipment.

METALWORKING: Gas weld/braze and cut. Sheetmetal layout, forming and assembly. Use of general machine shop tools.

AUTOMOBILE MECHANICS: Automotive maintenance, trouble shooting and repair.

EDUCATION:
Lee Grant High School
La Mesa, California
Graduate - 1987
Emphasis: Trade and Technical Courses

WORK EXPERIENCE:
1985 - 1987

M & M's Hamburgers
El Cajon, California
ASSISTANT MANAGER
Responsibilities: Supervised food line and cash register operation.

FOOD PROCESSOR

ACTIVITIES / ACHIEVEMENTS:
Run For Your Life Marathon Champion - 1986
Associated Student Body Representative - 1985 - 1986
Industrial Arts Student of the Year -1985
Industrial Arts Club Vice President - 1984 - 1985

REFERENCES:

Mr. Thomas A. Smith
Owner
M & M's Hamburgers
123 Second Avenue
El Cajon, California 92022
443-6689

Mrs. Dorothy Flint
Vice Principal
Lee Grant High School
540 University Avenue
La Mesa, California 92041
560-7790 (Extension 56)

Mr. Edward Lowell
Industrial Arts Instructor
Lee Grant High School
540 University Avenue
La Mesa, California 92041
560-790 (Extension 102)

Ms. Joyce Johnson
Attorney at Law
Wigley Building
2233 Indiana Avenue
Lakeside, California 92040
561-0099

EXAMPLE RESUME:
Technical Work Experience

EDWARD JAMES JONES
8972 Second Boulevard
Park Forest, Illinois 60466
(312) 747-7444
(312) 747-0200
(Message Number)

EMPLOYMENT GOAL:

To further develop my technical expertise involving mechanical/design applications including precision measuring and general machine operation/maintenance.

SKILLS:

Power/hand tool operation; reciprocal and centrifugal pump troubleshooting/repair and maintenance; chemical water analysis; gage calibration and maintenance; value rebuilding and maintenance; ability to utilize technical manuals; ability to utilize measuring tools (micrometer dial indicaors, vernier caliper); and utilization of manipulating mechanical devices (chain hoists, come-a-longs, prybars, etc.)

EXPERIENCE:
1982 - 1986

United States Navy — Honorable Discharge - December, 1986

BOILER TECHNICIAN (Petty Officer Third Class - E-4 Rating)

Responsibilities: Operation/maintenance of boilers and associated equipment including steam and electric pumps, fluid and heat transfer units, lighting off, maintenance watches, troubleshooting, emergency repair and damage control activities. Specialized servicing of fuel levels on ships; boiler water treatment; gage calibration; valve maintenance. Supervision of non-rated personnel.

1980 - 1982

Little Bear Company
Park Forest, Illinois
STOCK CLERK

EDUCATION:

United States Navy — San Diego, California
Boiler/Feed Water Testing and Treatment School - 1985
Gage Calibration School - 1985
Corrugated Ribbon Packing School - 1984
Boiler Technician Class A School - 1983

Prairie Community College
Chicago Heights, Illinois
12 units of General Education — 1982

Rich East High School
Park Forest, Illinois
Industrial Arts emphasis
Graduate — 1980

REFERENCES:

Available upon request as are Letters of Recommendation

EXAMPLE RESUME
Recent College Graduate

PERSONAL DATA SHEET

NAME: BETTY LOU SMITH

ADDRESS: 12 Central Avenue, #8
El Cajon, California 92020

TELEPHONE: (619) 579-1121
(619) 443-3311 - Message Number

SKILLS: Oral/written communications, public relations, retail sales/management, personnel supervision

EDUCATION: B.A., June, 1987, San Diego State University — San Diego, California
Major: Liberal Arts
Minor: Business

A.A., June, 1985, Northeastern College — Newland, Arizona
Major: Communications Arts

Bright Union High School — Newland, Arizona
Graduate — 1976

EXPERIENCE:

1985 - 1987 Marshall Company - San Diego, California

1986 - 1987 *CUSTOMER SERVICE MANAGER*
Responsibilities: Public relations, customer assistance/complaints, personnel supervision/scheduling.

1985 - 1986 *CUSTOMER SERVICE CLERK*
Responsibilities: Public relations, customer assistance/complaints.

1983 - 1985 Northeastern College — Newland, Arizona
COMMUNICATION ARTS DEPARTMENT AIDE
Responsibilities: Classroom instructor assistance involving visual aid presentations, paper correction, student assistance.

ACHIEVEMENTS: Employee of the Month — Marshall Company - 1987
Honor Graduate — San Diego State University - 1987
Arizona State Debate Champion — Northeastern College -1985

REFERENCES: Available upon request

COVER LETTERS

If you are applying for a job out-of-town or if you are unsuccessful in getting your name into a home town company via the telephone or visitation, the COVER LETTER may be for you.

WHAT IT IS:

A COVER LETTER is a professional and impressive written method of selling yourself.

PURPOSE:

The purpose of a COVER LETTER is to introduce your resume and/or employment application that is attached. A COVER LETTER can also be considered a letter of application. If you copy the example cover letter on page 223 by putting your own name and your own information in the appropriate places, you will have a perfect and acceptable COVER LETTER.

COVER LETTER POWER WORDS

If you are having difficulty with word choice in your cover letter, look over the COVER LETTER POWER WORDS provided on page 224.

EXAMPLE COVER LETTER

123 Bay Drive
San Diego, California 92010

September 1, 1986

Mr. George J. Webster
Director of Personnel
American Manufacturing Company
1323 Candy Lane
San Mateo, California 92123

Dear Mr. Webster:

I am interested in applying for employment as a Secretary/Receptionist.

I have excellent secretarial skills and have enclosed my resume for your consideration.

If American Manufacturing Company can utilize my skills and experience, please contact me at your earliest convenience for more information and/or an interview.

Thank you, in advance, for your consideration.

Very truly yours,

Mickey M. Moore

MICKEY M. MOORE
(714) 222-1022
(714) 222-11989 - Message Number

Enclosure

COVER LETTER POWER WORDS

The following are a few POWER WORDS you might use in your COVER LETTER:

accountability	expertise	qualifications
above	extensive	
advance		recent
advertisement	familiar	referenced
applicable	field	regarding
applying		related
appreciated	gentlemen	relocate
attached		response
available	information	resume
	interested	requested
background	interview	
	involving	seeking
capabilities		Sincerely yours,
comprehensive	know	skills
consideration	knowledge	specialize
contact		specific
continuous	Miss	
convenience	more	technical
currently	Mr.	techniques
	Mrs.	thank you
data sheet	Ms.	travel
Dear		
Dr.	open	understanding
	opportunity	
earliest		vacancy
emphasizing	particular	Very truly yours,
employment	plan	
enclosed	please	your
exemplifies	position	
experience	possible	
	production	

KEY CONCEPT

 The following are important points to remember about COVER LETTERS:

1. Follow the format exactly . . . adequate margins, good balance, short, neat, and always typewritten.

2. Send the COVER LETTER to a specific person. Never write "To Whom It May Concern" or "Dear Personnel Manager" if at all possible. Call the company you are applying to and get a name and title. An exception to this is when you are applying to a P.O. Box as advertised in a newspaper and no name or company is indicated. Then you may address correspondence to "Dear Personnel Manager."

3. The opening paragraph should be brief and to the point of why you are writing.

4. The second paragraph should be brief, touching on your work-related area(s) and referring to your enclosed resume.

5. The third paragraph should be brief. Reaffirm your interest in the company and request a response.

6. BE BRIEF. The entire body of the COVER LETTER should be contained in one page. Busy business people will not take the time nor the trouble to read a lengthy description of what is already included on your resume. They will appreciate your getting to the point.

SUMMARY

There are several different types of resumes and many books exist about writing them. However, most people can develop a very suitable and professional resume if they use the suggestions in this chapter. There are professional writing services available to you if you experience extreme difficulties in writing your own. Most services are costly, but can result in a good resume.

A cover letter is used when applying for out-of-town employment or when sending your resume and/or employment application through the mail. Send your cover letter to a specific person using his or her correct title. Be brief.

Remember . . . your resume and/or cover letter are a written picture of YOU so make them neat, concise, short, and to the point.

CHAPTER 10

After You Are Hired

KEEPING YOUR NEW JOB

GETTING A RAISE

JOB-CHANGING

TERMINATING TECHNIQUES

After You Are Hired

KEEPING YOUR NEW JOB

It takes a lot of work to get a job and it takes a lot of work to keep a job. During the probationary period you will have the opportunity to favorably impress your employer.

The probationary period is usually 30 days and merely means you can be let go with no recourse. The company just tries you out to see if you fit in. It is your job to see that you do fit in. The following are specific situations to be aware of so you can remain employed:

1. PUNCTUALITY: Many jobs are lost because people are late. Being late means late for work in the morning, late from breaks, or late from lunch. All are suicide.

2. ABSENTEEISM: To be absent from your new job is a sure way to lose it. Not showing up is worse than being late and creates tremendous hardships in a job situation. Not going to work causes more people to be fired than any other reason. If you must be absent, call in and tell your immediate supervisor why. When you return to work, thank your supervisor and apologize . . . even if the absence was justifiable.

3. GETTING ALONG: No matter what kind of job you get or what level of pay you earn, if you cannot get along with the people you work with, you will probably be let go. Remember, they hired you because they liked you . . . they will keep you because they like you. Respect your co-workers and expect their respect.

4. LISTEN AND RESPOND: Do what you are told (follow directions) and take notes if necessary. Rephrase directions in your own words to make sure you and your boss mutually understand what is to be done. (This is called feedback listening.)

5. RESPONSIBILITY: Be responsible. If you make a mistake, admit it openly and honestly. Mistakes are acceptable but dishonesty is not. Be responsible enough to correct an error. Being responsible does not mean knowing all the answers. It means knowing what you know and what you do *not* know.

6. COMMUNICATION: Always communicate positively. A glare from a driver you cut off on the highway is clear-cut communication — even at highway speeds. Your whole body talks and can give your attitudes away. Practice smiling, nodding your head to affirm what someone is saying, and making yourself look interested. Note-taking is a gesture that compliments people because it shows you are interested in what they say. Speak clearly, distinctly, and use standard English. Avoid bad language (cuss words) because you never know who you may offend.

7. LOYALTY: Develop faith in the company product. Loyalty is a must when you are employed. When you work for a company, the weak points are always obvious. Work at looking for the strong points because most organizations have both. If you dwell on the negative (weak points) you will lose faith and eventually become disenchanted. Unhappy working conditions and/or termination are the results. However, if you look for the positive (strong points) and attempt to improve the negative, your job performance will improve and you will progress in the company.

8. GOSSIP AND RUMORS: Rumors can cause tremendous internal strain and strife for a company . . . and for the employees. Rely only on information that comes "straight from the horse's mouth." When gossip begins, communication ends. Facts that are job-related are not gossip when shared with a supervisor for the purpose of increasing productivity. If unsure, the best rule to follow is: *If you can't say anything good . . . avoid saying anything.*"

9. ATTITUDE: It is better to learn than to know it all. Learning implies listening, following directions, and being moldable and compliant. Knowing it all implies lack of learning new ways and inflexibility. "Know-it-alls" generally get fired.

KEY CONCEPT

It took effort to get your job and it will take effort to keep it. If you avoid the pitfalls mentioned in this chapter and put in a good effort, you probably will never be fired. Even if you do not know everything about your job, your employer will appreciate you because of your obvious effort to learn.

GETTING A RAISE

After you have worked for 30 days (the usual probationary period), most companies have an automatic raise for the employees who are performing well, but this may not always be the case. Sometimes you must ask for a raise . . . you must assert yourself. Many bosses will respect you if you politely and assertively ask for what you want.

The following narrative will give you some ideas:

CAST:

Mickey: Hard-working (successful) employee

Mr. McScrooge: Employer

BEGIN:

Mickey: "Good Morning, Mr. McScrooge . . . may I chat with you for a minute?"

Mr. McScrooge: "Yes, Mickey . . . what can I do for you?"

Mickey: "I have been here 45 days and I feel I have performed well. I would like to discuss the possibility of a raise."

Mr. McScrooge: "I am glad you brought that up, Mickey. Do you feel a 40¢-an-hour increase would be fair compensation?"

Mickey: "I think that is most reasonable. Thank you for your understanding. Will that raise be reflected in my next paycheck?"

Mr. McScrooge: "Yes, I think that can be arranged. Have a nice day, Mickey."

Mickey: "You enjoy yours, too . . . and thanks for your understanding."

This conversation is somewhat idealistic, but reflects the best method of requesting a raise (or any other information) from an employer.

Know precisely what you want to say and say it. Be honest with yourself. If necessary, carry an itemized 3 × 5 card with you to insure you have covered all topics of importance.

Always begin your conversation with performance and relate that performance to the request for a raise. If you perform well, it is only reasonable to request that you be paid on that basis.

Even if you are not performing well, your boss should be able to tell you what to do so that you can get a raise.

Never request a raise because of inflation, personal needs, or pure desire . . . even the boss could always use more money. Stick to your PERFORMANCE as the reason.

KEY CONCEPT

Request raises ONLY on the basis of your performance. Be tactful but firm when requesting a raise and be prepared to negotiate the amount.

JOB-CHANGING

In the 1950's and 1960's we were socialized and taught never to quit a job. Job security was different and the job market was much more stable. Attitudes about job-retention and career-changing are different in our modern society.

It is projected that you will change jobs at least ten times in your lifetime. This includes both job changes in a specific career and actual career changes.

Because of our ever-changing technological society, many jobs that are sound today will be obsolete tomorrow. Terminating (quitting) a job does not mean that you are a quitter or a failure. Terminating can mean that you have elected to improve your status in life. How you terminate can have a tremendous impact on your future career success.

KEY CONCEPT

Job-changing is normal in today's modern society. Job security lies in you and your ability to perform.

TERMINATING TECHNIQUES

1. ALWAYS LEAVE ON GOOD TERMS

     Even if you did not like working for a company, it is always best to depart in a friendly manner and on good terms. You never know what twist of fate might force you to return and request employment with the same company at a later date. It is quite possible that the person you told off may change jobs too and be your boss at another company!

2. AVOID QUITTING UNTIL YOU HAVE
   ANOTHER JOB GUARANTEED

     Make sure your new position is secure (in writing if possible) before you give a termination notice to your current employer. You are always more employable when you are currently employed.

3. DO NOT TELL YOUR CURRENT EMPLOYER THAT YOU ARE SEEKING OTHER EMPLOYMENT

Some employers may apply pressure or even let you go if they know you are actively seeking another job. It is your personal business if you are applying at other companies and you are not obligated to inform your current employer. Request the company that you are interviewing with not to contact your current employer without your permission. Your current employment status is a recommendation in itself. After applying and comparing companies, you may discover that the company you are working for is not so bad after all.

4. GIVE TWO WEEKS QUITTING NOTICE, IF POSSIBLE

Always give your present employer written notification that you are going to quit (a handwritten note will do). Two weeks is usually a comfortable time span, but often one week is enough.

If your new employer wants you to begin work sooner than a two-week quitting notice will allow, you may be able to negotiate with your present employer regarding the termination date. Avoid making promises to your new employer until you have discussed your termination date with your present employer. Both will respect you for this consideration.

5. REQUEST A LETTER OF RECOMMENDATION

If you have been a satisfactory employee, quitting for various reasons is perfectly acceptable and often admired.

Before you actually leave, request a LETTER OF RECOMMENDATION to take with you. You may want a LETTER OF RECOMMENDATION the following year only to find the company out-of-business or, believe it or not, they may have forgotten who you are!

The letter's salutation should read, "To Whom It May Concern." It should be typed or written on company letterhead stationery. You may even indicate (in a memo) what specific items you want mentioned in the letter. You may even type the letter yourself ahead of time and present it to your current employer for signature. The letter then becomes part of your personal employment package that can be used whenever you decide to change jobs. This personal employment package contains all information pertinent to job-seeking.

The following is a sample LETTER OF RECOMMENDATION:

EXAMPLE LETTER OF RECOMMENDATION
(To be typed on letterhead stationery)

WE-CAN-DO MANUFACTURING

August 28, 1986

To Whom It May Concern:

This is a letter of introduction and recommendation for Mickey Moore, who has been successfully employed by We-Can-Do Manufacturing Company from June, 1978 through August, 1986.

Mickey was the Secretary for the Marketing Department and always worked above expected standards. Her clerical skills are excellent but she is especially effective in public relations. Detail work (billing, proposals, etc.) was always well done. Ms. Moore was always punctual and rarely missed a day of work.

I highly recommend that Ms. Moore be hired for any clerical/secretarial position. Her termination status with We-Can-Do Manufacturing Company is very rehirable.

Sincerely,

Thomas P. Weber

THOMAS P. WEBER
Vice President - Marketing

TPW/ccl

341 Rosewood Drive • San Diego, California 92013 • (714) 222-7644

KEY CONCEPT

TERMINATE (quit) a job in a manner that shows what a good employee you are. Obtain a letter of recommendation BEFORE leaving a current position. Use the given TECHNIQUES for successful terminating skills and good future references.

SUMMARY

Keep your new job by avoiding the common employment pitfalls.

Raises are earned on the basis of performance and should be requested accordingly from your employer.

Changing jobs is acceptable if you leave on good terms and give reasonable quitting notice. Request a letter of recommendation upon termination. Make sure your new job is assured before quitting your old one.

Final Comment

*Nothing in the world can take the place of
persistence.*

*Talent will not . . . nothing is more common
than unsuccessful men with talent.*

*Genius will not . . . unrewarded genius is
almost a proverb.*

*Education alone will not . . . the world is full
of educated derelicts.*

*PERSISTENCE and DETERMINATION
alone are omnipotent.*

—Calvin Coolidge

JOB-SEEKING

TOOLS

APPLICATION INFORMATION TOOL
(Page 1 of 3)

NAME: _____
        (Last)   (First)   (Middle)

ADDRESS: _____
         (Street)   (City)   (State)   (Zip)

PHONE NUMBER: _____ _____

           _____ _____
                   (Message Number)

SOCIAL SECURITY NUMBER: _____

DRIVER'S LICENSE NUMBER: _____

EDUCATION:

  Grade School: Years Attended: Degree:
_____

_____

  High School   Years Attended: Degree:
_____

_____

_____

  College: Years Attended: Degree:
_____

_____

_____

_____

  Trade, Business, Correspondence: Years Attended: Degree:
_____

_____

_____

_____

  Special Study, Research, Apprenticeships, On-the-job training:
_____

_____

_____

_____

_____

_____

APPLICATION INFORMATION TOOL
(Page 2 of 3)

EMPLOYMENT HISTORY:

Company Name: _____

Address: _____

Position: _____

Duties: _____

_____

Supervisor: _____ Title: _____

Starting Date: _____

Termination Date: _____

Reason for Leaving: _____

Hourly Wage: _____

Company Name: _____

Address: _____

Position: _____

Duties: _____

_____

Supervisor: _____ Title: _____

Starting Date: _____

Termination Date: _____

Reason for Leaving: _____

Hourly Wage: _____

Company Name: _____

Address: _____

Position: _____

Duties: _____

_____

Supervisor: _____ Title: _____

Starting Date: _____

Termination Date: _____

Reason for Leaving: _____

Hourly Wage: _____

APPLICATION INFORMATION TOOL
(Page 3 of 3)

MILITARY SERVICE:

    Branch: _____ Dates: _____

    Rate/Rank Upon Discharge: _____

    Job Description: _____

    Discharge: _____

JOB YOU ARE APPLYING FOR:

_____

ANTICIPATED SALARY:

_____

PROFESSIONAL ORGANIZATIONS:

_____

REFERENCES: _____

    Name

    Title

    Company Name

    Address

    City   State   Zip

    Area Code   Telephone Number

    Name

    Title

    Company Name

    Address

    City   State   Zip

    Area Code   Telephone Number

POUNDING THE PAVEMENT TOOL

1. Date: _____ Company/Firm Name: _____

   Address: _____

   Contact Person: _____ Phone: _____

   ☐ Follow-Up   ☐ Application   ☐ Resume   ☐ Interview

2. Date: _____ Company/Firm Name: _____

   Address: _____

   Contact Person: _____ Phone: _____

   ☐ Follow-Up   ☐ Application   ☐ Resume   ☐ Interview

3. Date: _____ Company/Firm Name: _____

   Address: _____

   Contact Person: _____ Phone: _____

   ☐ Follow-Up   ☐ Application   ☐ Resume   ☐ Interview

4. Date: _____ Company/Firm Name: _____

   Address: _____

   Contact Person: _____ Phone: _____

   ☐ Follow-Up   ☐ Application   ☐ Resume   ☐ Interview

5. Date: _____ Company/Firm Name: _____

   Address: _____

   Contact Person: _____ Phone: _____

   ☐ Follow-Up   ☐ Application   ☐ Resume   ☐ Interview

6. Date: _____ Company/Firm Name: _____

   Address: _____

   Contact Person: _____ Phone: _____

   ☐ Follow-Up   ☐ Application   ☐ Resume   ☐ Interview

7. Date: _____ Company/Firm Name: _____

   Address: _____

   Contact Person: _____ Phone: _____

   ☐ Follow-Up   ☐ Application   ☐ Resume   ☐ Interview

POUNDING THE PAVEMENT TOOL

1. Date: _____ Company/Firm Name: _____

    Address: _____

    Contact Person: _____ Phone: _____

    ☐ Follow-Up   ☐ Application   ☐ Resume   ☐ Interview

2. Date: _____ Company/Firm Name: _____

    Address: _____

    Contact Person: _____ Phone: _____

    ☐ Follow-Up   ☐ Application   ☐ Resume   ☐ Interview

3. Date: _____ Company/Firm Name: _____

    Address: _____

    Contact Person: _____ Phone: _____

    ☐ Follow-Up   ☐ Application   ☐ Resume   ☐ Interview

4. Date: _____ Company/Firm Name: _____

    Address: _____

    Contact Person: _____ Phone: _____

    ☐ Follow-Up   ☐ Application   ☐ Resume   ☐ Interview

5. Date: _____ Company/Firm Name: _____

    Address: _____

    Contact Person: _____ Phone: _____

    ☐ Follow-Up   ☐ Application   ☐ Resume   ☐ Interview

6. Date: _____ Company/Firm Name: _____

    Address: _____

    Contact Person: _____ Phone: _____

    ☐ Follow-Up   ☐ Application   ☐ Resume   ☐ Interview

7. Date: _____ Company/Firm Name: _____

    Address: _____

    Contact Person: _____ Phone: _____

    ☐ Follow-Up   ☐ Application   ☐ Resume   ☐ Interview

POUNDING THE PAVEMENT TOOL

1. Date: _____ Company/Firm Name: _____
   Address: _____
   Contact Person: _____ Phone: _____
   ☐ Follow-Up   ☐ Application   ☐ Resume   ☐ Interview

2. Date: _____ Company/Firm Name: _____ _____
   Address: _____
   Contact Person: _____Phone: _____
   ☐ Follow-Up   ☐ Application   ☐ Resume   ☐ Interview

3. Date: _____ Company/Firm Name: _____
   Address: _____
   Contact Person: _____ Phone: _____
   ☐ Follow-Up   ☐ Application   ☐ Resume   ☐ Interview

4. Date: _____ Company/Firm Name: _____
   Address: _____
   Contact Person: _____ Phone: _____
   ☐ Follow-Up   ☐ Application   ☐ Resume   ☐ Interview

5. Date: _____ Company/Firm Name: _____
   Address: _____
   Contact Person: _____Phone: _____
   ☐ Follow-Up   ☐ Application   ☐ Resume   ☐ Interview

6. Date: _____ Company/Firm Name: _____
   Address: _____
   Contact Person: _____ Phone: _____
   ☐ Follow-Up   ☐ Application   ☐ Resume   ☐ Interview

7. Date: _____ Company/Firm Name: _____
   Address: _____
   Contact Person: _____ Phone: _____
   ☐ Follow-Up   ☐ Application   ☐ Resume   ☐ Interview

POUNDING THE PAVEMENT TOOL

1. Date: _____ Company/Firm Name: _____
   Address: _____
   Contact Person: _____ Phone: _____
   ☐ Follow-Up ☐ Application ☐ Resume ☐ Interview

2. Date: _____ Company/Firm Name: _____
   Address: _____
   Contact Person: _____ Phone: _____
   ☐ Follow-Up ☐ Application ☐ Resume ☐ Interview

3. Date: _____ Company/Firm Name: _____
   Address: _____
   Contact Person: _____ Phone: _____
   ☐ Follow-Up ☐ Application ☐ Resume ☐ Interview

4. Date: _____ Company/Firm Name: _____
   Address: _____
   Contact Person: _____ Phone: _____
   ☐ Follow-Up ☐ Application ☐ Resume ☐ Interview

5. Date: _____ Company/Firm Name: _____
   Address: _____
   Contact Person: _____ Phone: _____
   ☐ Follow-Up ☐ Application ☐ Resume ☐ Interview

6. Date: _____ Company/Firm Name: _____
   Address: _____
   Contact Person: _____ Phone: _____
   ☐ Follow-Up ☐ Application ☐ Resume ☐ Interview

7. Date: _____ Company/Firm Name: _____
   Address: _____
   Contact Person: _____ Phone: _____
   ☐ Follow-Up ☐ Application ☐ Resume ☐ Interview

POUNDING THE PAVEMENT TOOL

1. Date: _____ Company/Firm Name: _____
   Address: _____
   Contact Person: _____ Phone: _____
   ☐ Follow-Up   ☐ Application   ☐ Resume   ☐ Interview

2. Date: _____ Company/Firm Name: _____
   Address: _____
   Contact Person: _____Phone: _____
   ☐ Follow-Up   ☐ Application   ☐ Resume   ☐ Interview

3. Date: _____ Company/Firm Name: _____
   Address: _____
   Contact Person: _____ Phone: _____
   ☐ Follow-Up   ☐ Application   ☐ Resume   ☐ Interview

4. Date: _____ Company/Firm Name: _____
   Address: _____
   Contact Person: _____ Phone: _____
   ☐ Follow-Up   ☐ Application   ☐ Resume   ☐ Interview

5. Date: _____ Company/Firm Name: _____
   Address: _____
   Contact Person: _____Phone: _____
   ☐ Follow-Up   ☐ Application   ☐ Resume   ☐ Interview

6. Date: _____ Company/Firm Name: _____
   Address: _____
   Contact Person: _____ Phone: _____
   ☐ Follow-Up   ☐ Application   ☐ Resume   ☐ Interview

7. Date: _____ Company/Firm Name: _____
   Address: _____
   Contact Person: _____ Phone: _____
   ☐ Follow-Up   ☐ Application   ☐ Resume   ☐ Interview

PHONE SEARCH TOOL

COMPANY	PERSON	PHONE	NOTHING AVAILABLE	CALL BACK	SEND RESUME	APPLICATION	INTERVIEW
							FILL OUT TOP SECTION OF **INTERVIEW INFORMATION TOOL**

PHONE SEARCH TOOL

COMPANY	PERSON	PHONE	NOTHING AVAILABLE	CALL BACK	SEND RESUME	APPLICATION	INTERVIEW
							FILL OUT TOP SECTION OF **INTERVIEW INFORMATION TOOL**

PHONE SEARCH TOOL

COMPANY	PERSON	PHONE	NOTHING AVAILABLE	CALL BACK	SEND RESUME	APPLICATION	INTERVIEW
							FILL OUT TOP SECTION OF **INTERVIEW INFORMATION TOOL**

PHONE SEARCH TOOL

COMPANY	PERSON	PHONE	NOTHING AVAILABLE	CALL BACK	SEND RESUME	APPLICATION	INTERVIEW
							FILL OUT TOP SECTION OF **INTERVIEW INFORMATION TOOL**

PHONE SEARCH TOOL

COMPANY	PERSON	PHONE	NOTHING AVAILABLE	CALL BACK	SEND RESUME	APPLICATION	INTERVIEW
						FILL OUT TOP SECTION OF **INTERVIEW INFORMATION TOOL**	

PHONE SCRIPT TOOL

AFTER YOU DIAL THE PHONE AND THE COMPANY HAS RESPONDED:

Hello, my name is _____ .

Who is the person in charge of hiring? _____

Will you spell his name for me, please? _____

May I speak to _____ , please. Thank you.

AFTER THE CONNECTION HAS BEEN MADE:

Hello, _____ . My name is _____ .

(RESPONSE #1)

I have _____ years experience as _____ .

I am interested in a position with your company.

or

(RESPONSE #2)

I have just completed a vocational training program and have _____

_____ entry level skills.

I _____

I am interested in any entry level _____

position you might have available.

or

(RESPONSE #3)

I am interested in applying for any entry level _____

_____ position you might have available.

IF POSITIVE RESPONSE:

Fill in top section of INTERVIEW INFORMATION TOOL.

IF NEGATIVE RESPONSE:

May I come in and fill out an application or send you my resume?

☐ YES RESPONSE: When would be a good time to come in?_____

☐ NO RESPONSE: May I call you again . . . say in a couple weeks? _____

Do you know of any company with openings at this time that could benefit from my
skills? _____

Thank you very much for your time and consideration. I hope to talk to you again.

PHONE SCRIPT TOOL

AFTER YOU DIAL THE PHONE AND THE COMPANY HAS RESPONDED:

Hello, my name is _____ .

Who is the person in charge of hiring? _____

Will you spell his name for me, please? _____

May I speak to _____ , please. Thank you.

AFTER THE CONNECTION HAS BEEN MADE:

Hello, _____ . My name is _____ .

(RESPONSE #1)

I have _____ years experience as _____ .

I am interested in a position with your company.

or

(RESPONSE #2)

I have just completed a vocational training program and have _____

_____ entry level skills.

I _____

I am interested in any entry level _____

position you might have available.

or

(RESPONSE #3)

I am interested in applying for any entry level _____

_____position you might have available.

IF POSITIVE RESPONSE:

Fill in top section of INTERVIEW INFORMATION TOOL.

IF NEGATIVE RESPONSE:

May I come in and fill out an application or send you my resume?

☐ YES RESPONSE: When would be a good time to come in?_____

☐ NO RESPONSE: May I call you again . . . say in a couple weeks? _____

Do you know of any company with openings at this time that could benefit from my skills? _____

Thank you very much for your time and consideration. I hope to talk to you again.

PHONE SCRIPT TOOL

AFTER YOU DIAL THE PHONE AND THE COMPANY HAS RESPONDED:

Hello, my name is _____ .

Who is the person in charge of hiring? _____

Will you spell his name for me, please? _____

May I speak to _____ , please. Thank you.

AFTER THE CONNECTION HAS BEEN MADE:

Hello, _____ . My name is _____ .

(RESPONSE #1)

I have _____ years experience as _____ .

I am interested in a position with your company.

or

(RESPONSE #2)

I have just completed a vocational training program and have _____

_____ entry level skills.

I _____

I am interested in any entry level _____

position you might have available.

or

(RESPONSE #3)

I am interested in applying for any entry level _____

_____ position you might have available.

IF POSITIVE RESPONSE:

Fill in top section of INTERVIEW INFORMATION TOOL.

IF NEGATIVE RESPONSE:

May I come in and fill out an application or send you my resume?

☐ YES RESPONSE: When would be a good time to come in?_____

☐ NO RESPONSE: May I call you again . . . say in a couple weeks? _____

Do you know of any company with openings at this time that could benefit from my skills? _____

Thank you very much for your time and consideration. I hope to talk to you again.

PHONE SCRIPT TOOL

AFTER YOU DIAL THE PHONE AND THE COMPANY HAS RESPONDED:

Hello, my name is _____.

Who is the person in charge of hiring? _____

Will you spell his name for me, please? _____

May I speak to _____, please. Thank you.

AFTER THE CONNECTION HAS BEEN MADE:

Hello, _____. My name is _____.

(RESPONSE #1)

I have _____ years experience as _____.

I am interested in a position with your company.

or

(RESPONSE #2)

I have just completed a vocational training program and have _____

_____ entry level skills.

I _____

I am interested in any entry level _____

position you might have available.

or

(RESPONSE #3)

I am interested in applying for any entry level _____

_____position you might have available.

IF POSITIVE RESPONSE:

Fill in top section of INTERVIEW INFORMATION TOOL.

IF NEGATIVE RESPONSE:

May I come in and fill out an application or send you my resume?

☐ YES RESPONSE: When would be a good time to come in?_____

☐ NO RESPONSE: May I call you again . . . say in a couple weeks? _____

Do you know of any company with openings at this time that could benefit from my skills? _____

Thank you very much for your time and consideration. I hope to talk to you again.

PHONE SCRIPT TOOL

AFTER YOU DIAL THE PHONE AND THE COMPANY HAS RESPONDED:

Hello, my name is _____

Who is the person in charge of hiring? _____

Will you spell his name for me, please? _____

May I speak to _____ , please. Thank you.

AFTER THE CONNECTION HAS BEEN MADE:

Hello, _____ . My name is _____ .

(RESPONSE #1)

I have _____ years experience as _____ .

I am interested in a position with your company.

or

(RESPONSE #2)

I have just completed a vocational training program and have _____

_____ entry level skills.

I _____

I am interested in any entry level _____

position you might have available.

or

(RESPONSE #3)

I am interested in applying for any entry level _____

_____position you might have available.

IF POSITIVE RESPONSE:

Fill in top section of INTERVIEW INFORMATION TOOL.

IF NEGATIVE RESPONSE:

May I come in and fill out an application or send you my resume?

☐ YES RESPONSE: When would be a good time to come in?_____

☐ NO RESPONSE: May I call you again . . . say in a couple weeks? _____

Do you know of any company with openings at this time that could benefit from my skills? _____

Thank you very much for your time and consideration. I hope to talk to you again.

INTERVIEW INFORMATION TOOL

WHAT YOU MUST KNOW **BEFORE** THE INTERVIEW:

Day: _____ Date: _____ Time: _____

Company Name: _____

Address:_____

Interviewer's Name: _____ Title: _____

Room Number: _____ Phone Number: _____ Extension: _____

Transportation: _____ Parking: _____

Major Facts About the Company: _____

_____

Job You Want at This Company: _____

WHAT YOU MUST ASK **DURING** THE INTERVIEW:

Jobs Discussed During the Interview: _____

Job Duties:_____

Rate of Pay: _____

Raises/Pay/Increases: _____

Fringe Benefits:_____

Opportunities for Advancement: _____

On-The-Job Training: _____

Work Schedule:_____

Breaks: _____ Lunch: _____

When Will I Know?_____

May I Call You? _____ When? _____

THANK YOU.

Notes:_____

_____

_____

_____

_____

_____

_____

_____

INTERVIEW INFORMATION TOOL

WHAT YOU MUST KNOW **BEFORE** THE INTERVIEW:

Day: _____ Date: _____ Time: _____

Company Name: _____

Address:_____

Interviewer's Name: _____ Title: _____

Room Number: _____ Phone Number: _____ Extension: _____

Transportation: _____ Parking: _____

Major Facts About the Company: _____

_____

Job You Want at This Company: _____

WHAT YOU MUST ASK **DURING** THE INTERVIEW:

Jobs Discussed During the Interview: _____

Job Duties: _____

Rate of Pay: _____

Raises/Pay/Increases: _____

Fringe Benefits: _____

Opportunities for Advancement: _____

On-The-Job Training: _____

Work Schedule: _____

Breaks: _____ Lunch: _____

When Will I Know?_____

May I Call You? _____ When? _____

THANK YOU.

Notes:_____

_____

_____

_____

_____

_____

_____

INTERVIEW INFORMATION TOOL

WHAT YOU MUST KNOW **BEFORE** THE INTERVIEW:

Day: _____ Date: _____ Time: _____

Company Name: _____

Address:_____

Interviewer's Name: _____ Title: _____

Room Number: _____ Phone Number: _____ Extension: _____

Transportation: _____ Parking: _____

Major Facts About the Company: _____

_____

Job You Want at This Company: _____

WHAT YOU MUST ASK **DURING** THE INTERVIEW:

Jobs Discussed During the Interview: _____

Job Duties:_____

Rate of Pay: _____

Raises/Pay/Increases: _____

Fringe Benefits:_____

Opportunities for Advancement: _____

On-The-Job Training: _____

Work Schedule:_____

Breaks: _____ Lunch: _____

When Will I Know?_____

May I Call You? _____ When? _____

THANK YOU.

Notes:_____

_____

_____

_____

_____

_____

_____

INTERVIEW INFORMATION TOOL

WHAT YOU MUST KNOW **BEFORE** THE INTERVIEW:

Day: _____ Date: _____ Time: _____

Company Name: _____

Address: _____

Interviewer's Name: _____ Title: _____

Room Number: _____ Phone Number: _____ Extension: _____

Transportation: _____ Parking: _____

Major Facts About the Company: _____

_____

Job You Want at This Company: _____

WHAT YOU MUST ASK **DURING** THE INTERVIEW:

Jobs Discussed During the Interview: _____

Job Duties: _____

Rate of Pay: _____

Raises/Pay/Increases: _____

Fringe Benefits: _____

Opportunities for Advancement: _____

On-The-Job Training: _____

Work Schedule: _____

Breaks: _____ Lunch: _____

When Will I Know? _____

May I Call You? _____ When? _____

THANK YOU.

Notes: _____

_____

_____

_____

_____

_____

_____

INTERVIEW INFORMATION TOOL

WHAT YOU MUST KNOW **BEFORE** THE INTERVIEW:

Day: _____ Date: _____ Time: _____

Company Name: _____

Address: _____

Interviewer's Name: _____ Title: _____

Room Number: _____ Phone Number: _____ Extension: _____

Transportation: _____ Parking: _____

Major Facts About the Company: _____

_____

Job You Want at This Company: _____

WHAT YOU MUST ASK **DURING** THE INTERVIEW:

Jobs Discussed During the Interview: _____

Job Duties: _____

Rate of Pay: _____

Raises/Pay/Increases: _____

Fringe Benefits: _____

Opportunities for Advancement: _____

On-The-Job Training: _____

Work Schedule: _____

Breaks: _____ Lunch: _____

When Will I Know? _____

May I Call You? _____ When? _____

THANK YOU.

Notes: _____

_____

_____

_____

_____

_____

_____ _____

_____

INTERVIEW INFORMATION TOOL

WHAT YOU MUST KNOW **BEFORE** THE INTERVIEW:

Day: _____ Date: _____ Time: _____

Company Name: _____

Address:_____

Interviewer's Name: _____ Title: _____

Room Number: _____ Phone Number: _____ Extension: _____

Transportation: _____ Parking: _____

Major Facts About the Company: _____

_____

Job You Want at This Company: _____

WHAT YOU MUST ASK **DURING** THE INTERVIEW:

Jobs Discussed During the Interview: _____

Job Duties:_____

Rate of Pay: _____

Raises/Pay/Increases: _____

Fringe Benefits:_____

Opportunities for Advancement:_____

On-The-Job Training: _____

Work Schedule:_____

Breaks: _____ Lunch: _____

When Will I Know?_____

May I Call You? _____ When? _____

THANK YOU.

Notes:_____

_____

_____

_____

_____

_____

_____

INTERVIEW INFORMATION TOOL

WHAT YOU MUST KNOW **BEFORE** THE INTERVIEW:

Day: _____ Date: _____ Time: _____

Company Name: _____

Address:_____

Interviewer's Name: _____ Title: _____

Room Number: _____ Phone Number: _____ Extension: _____

Transportation: _____ Parking: _____

Major Facts About the Company: _____

_____

Job You Want at This Company: _____

WHAT YOU MUST ASK **DURING** THE INTERVIEW:

Jobs Discussed During the Interview: _____

Job Duties:_____

Rate of Pay: _____

Raises/Pay/Increases: _____

Fringe Benefits:_____

Opportunities for Advancement:_____

On-The-Job Training: _____

Work Schedule:_____

Breaks: _____ Lunch: _____

When Will I Know?_____

May I Call You? _____ When? _____

THANK YOU.

Notes:_____

_____

_____

_____

_____

_____

_____

INTERVIEW INFORMATION TOOL

WHAT YOU MUST KNOW **BEFORE** THE INTERVIEW:

Day: _____ Date: _____ Time: _____

Company Name: _____

Address:_____

Interviewer's Name: _____ Title: _____

Room Number: _____ Phone Number: _____ Extension: _____

Transportation: _____ Parking: _____

Major Facts About the Company: _____

_____

Job You Want at This Company: _____

WHAT YOU MUST ASK **DURING** THE INTERVIEW:

Jobs Discussed During the Interview: _____

Job Duties:_____

Rate of Pay: _____

Raises/Pay/Increases: _____

Fringe Benefits:_____

Opportunities for Advancement: _____

On-The-Job Training: _____

Work Schedule:_____

Breaks: _____ Lunch: _____

When Will I Know?_____

May I Call You? _____ When? _____

THANK YOU.

Notes:_____

_____

_____

_____

_____

_____

_____

INTERVIEW INFORMATION TOOL

WHAT YOU MUST KNOW **BEFORE** THE INTERVIEW:

Day: _____ Date: _____ Time: _____

Company Name: _____

Address:_____

Interviewer's Name: _____ Title: _____

Room Number: _____ Phone Number: _____ Extension: _____

Transportation: _____ Parking: _____

Major Facts About the Company: _____

_____

Job You Want at This Company: _____

WHAT YOU MUST ASK **DURING** THE INTERVIEW:

Jobs Discussed During the Interview: _____

Job Duties:_____

Rate of Pay: _____

Raises/Pay/Increases: _____

Fringe Benefits:_____

Opportunities for Advancement: _____

On-The-Job Training: _____

Work Schedule:_____

Breaks: _____ Lunch: _____

When Will I Know?_____

May I Call You? _____ When? _____

THANK YOU.

Notes:_____

_____

_____

_____

_____

_____

_____

INTERVIEW INFORMATION TOOL

WHAT YOU MUST KNOW **BEFORE** THE INTERVIEW:

Day: _____ Date: _____ Time: _____

Company Name: _____

Address: _____

Interviewer's Name: _____ Title: _____

Room Number: _____ Phone Number: _____ Extension: _____

Transportation: _____ Parking: _____

Major Facts About the Company: _____

_____

Job You Want at This Company: _____

WHAT YOU MUST ASK **DURING** THE INTERVIEW:

Jobs Discussed During the Interview: _____

Job Duties: _____

Rate of Pay: _____

Raises/Pay/Increases: _____

Fringe Benefits: _____

Opportunities for Advancement: _____

On-The-Job Training: _____

Work Schedule: _____

Breaks: _____ Lunch: _____

When Will I Know? _____

May I Call You? _____ When? _____

THANK YOU.

Notes: _____

_____

_____

_____

_____

_____

_____

INTERVIEW INFORMATION TOOL

WHAT YOU MUST KNOW **BEFORE** THE INTERVIEW:

Day: _____ Date: _____ Time: _____

Company Name: _____

Address: _____

Interviewer's Name: _____ Title: _____

Room Number: _____ Phone Number: _____ Extension: _____

Transportation: _____ Parking: _____

Major Facts About the Company: _____

_____

Job You Want at This Company: _____

WHAT YOU MUST ASK **DURING** THE INTERVIEW:

Jobs Discussed During the Interview: _____

Job Duties: _____

Rate of Pay: _____

Raises/Pay/Increases: _____

Fringe Benefits: _____

Opportunities for Advancement: _____

On-The-Job Training: _____

Work Schedule: _____

Breaks: _____ Lunch: _____

When Will I Know? _____

May I Call You? _____ When? _____

THANK YOU.

Notes: _____

_____

_____

_____

_____

_____

_____

RESUME TOOL
(Page 1 of 3)

NAME: _____

ADDRESS: _____

TELEPHONE NUMBER: _____ _____

MESSAGE NUMBER: _____ _____

SKILLS: _____

_____

_____

EXPERIENCE:

_____ to _____ _____
                Company Name

                _____
                City   State   Zip

                _____
                Your Title

                _____
                Your Responsibilities and/or duties

                _____

                _____

                _____

_____ to _____ _____
                Company Name

                _____
                City   State   Zip

                _____
                Your Title

                _____
                Your Responsibilities and/or duties

                _____

                _____

                _____

RESUME TOOL
(Page 2 of 3)

EDUCATION:
(Most recent first)   School Name

City   State

Degree — Certificate — Courses — Units — Workshops, etc.

Year Attended
(Graduated)

School Name

City   State

Degree — Certificate — Courses — Units — Workshops, etc.

Year Attended
(Graduated)

School Name

City   State

Degree — Certificate — Courses — Units — Workshops, etc.

Year Attended
(Graduated)

ACHIEVEMENTS:
(Optional)

Hobbies:
(Optional —
depending on
room available)

REFERENCES: Available on request

RESUME TOOL
(Page 3 of 3)

REFERENCES: _____
Name

_____
Title

_____
Company Name

_____
Address

_____ _____ _____
City   State   Zip

_____ _____
Area Code   Telephone Number

_____
Name

_____
Title

_____
Company Name

_____
Address

_____ _____ _____
City   State   Zip

_____ _____
Area Code   Telephone Number

_____
Name

_____
Title

_____
Company Name

_____
Address

_____ _____ _____
City   State   Zip

_____ _____
Area Code   Telephone Number

INDEX